KINGDOM HUSTLE
*Pursuing Purpose
Over Paychecks*

Copyright © 2025 Derek Stone
All rights reserved.

No part of this publication may be reproduced, stored in a retrieval system, or transmitted in any form or by any means: electronic, mechanical, photocopying, recording, or otherwise, without the prior written permission of the author, except for brief quotations used in reviews or scholarly works.

Scripture quotations are taken from the Holy Bible, New International Version®, NIV®. Copyright ©1973, 1978, 1984, 2011 by Biblica, Inc.™ Used by permission. All rights reserved worldwide.

Cover design created by the author.
Interior layout by the author.

Printed in the United States of America
First Edition: 2025
ISBN: 979-8-993857-2-0

To my wife, Alicia, my rock, my anchor, and the fiercest support I've ever known. You've carried more than anyone sees and loved me through every chapter.

ACKNOWLEDGMENTS

First and foremost, to King Jesus: this book is Yours. Every word, every idea, every insight has been shaped by Your voice, Your mercy, and Your Spirit. I only build because You first called.

To my wife, Alicia: thank you for being my constant. Your strength anchors me, your encouragement fuels me, and your quiet support gives me the confidence to keep building.

To my children: you inspire me to build something worth handing down. You're the reason I fight to lead with integrity and build something that lasts. I pray you see in me a man who obeyed God more than he chased applause.

To the friends and mentors who've sharpened me along the way: your wisdom and accountability have helped me stay faithful when it would've been easier to slip.

To every business owner, builder, or Kingdom-minded leader who has shared their story with me, encouraged me, or reminded me why this message matters; thank you.

Finally, to every reader who chooses to build God's way, I see you, I honor you, and I'm praying this book fans the flame inside you.

Let's build what matters.

FOREWORD

I met Derek when my wife and I left security to follow God into a new state and a new business. God showed His faithfulness through people, and Derek quickly became a mentor, partner, and trusted friend.

Derek leads by example as a business owner, host of The ARC Entrepreneur Podcast, and facilitator of his church's entrepreneur club. Together we've watched many Christian entrepreneurs start with a God-given dream and drift into a self-driven empire.

That's why this book is so important.

Kingdom Hustle isn't a "10 steps on how to make more money" book. It's a prophetic wake-up call to remember why you started, and Who sent you. It's also a call to return to a mindset of value over money, where integrity matters more than speed, and service is more important than self.

Ironically, that mindset doesn't just lead to deeper impact, it leads to greater returns and a business that lasts.

Kingdom hustle isn't about grinding for gain. It's about stewarding the gift and doing the work with clean hands, clear eyes, and eternity in mind.

If you're a business owner, entrepreneur, leader, or visionary who's tired of the noise and hungry for what's real, this is for you.

If you've ever felt the tension between **paychecks and purpose**, this is for you.

Daniel Callahan
ARC Entrepreneur Podcast
Callahan & Co. Real Estate

TABLE OF CONTENTS

Section One — Breaking the Cultural Illusion

Chapter One: The Myth of the Side Hustle	12
Chapter Two: Kingdom Over Culture	23
Chapter Three: Work Was God's First Assignment	32
Chapter Four: The King's Assignment	41

Section Two — Building with Kingdom Vision

Chapter Five: Vision Over Virality	52
Chapter Six: Seed, Not Speed	63
Chapter Seven: Obedience Over Opportunity	71
Chapter Eight: Marketplace Ministry	82

Section Three — Expanding with Kingdom Purpose

Chapter Nine: Provision Follows Purpose	93
Chapter Ten: Anointed to Build	102
Chapter Eleven: Warfare in the Work	113
Chapter Twelve: Don't Build	121
Chapter Thirteen: Legacy Over Likes	129
Conclusion: The Commissioning	138

INTRODUCTION

Called to Build Differently

I'll never forget the moment that changed everything.

It started with a simple question I asked my boss at the time:

"What do you think of me?"

He looked at me with a half-smile and replied, "I'm not so sure you want to know?"

Confident, maybe too confident, I said, "Of course I do."

His response crushed my ego but saved my soul:
"I like you, but you're replaceable. You're just like all the others."

"Whoa!" Those words hit like a gut punch. I thought I was exceptional. I thought I was winning.

What I heard forced me to take a hard look in the mirror.

If I were honest with myself, deep down, I knew he was right.

That conversation didn't just bruise my pride, it exposed it. It sparked a fire in me, not one of performance, but of purpose. It revealed the emptiness of my hustle and awakened a hunger for something more.

From that day on, I decided: I would become the hardest worker in the room, not for applause, but for impact.

We live in a world that glamorizes busyness.

"Rise and grind."
"No days off."
"Secure the bag."

"Make your side hustle your main hustle."

Here's the truth no one's posting:

Hustle without Heaven is just noise.
Grind without God is just burnout waiting to happen.
Chasing success without calling is a race to nowhere.

There's a better way.
A higher way.
A Kingdom way.

Kingdom Hustle means we work, but not like the world.

It's not about "chasing the bag".
It's about chasing God's purpose.

It means putting Christ first in everything:

Every decision.
Every act.
Every word.

It means we measure success differently.
Not just by revenue, but by eternal return.

I run a very successful business, but our bottom line doesn't always look like conventional success, and that's intentional.

We don't chase fast profit. We pursue lasting value.

Adding it. Giving it. Multiplying it. Sometimes that's cost us in the short term.

However, in the long term, wow! It's built something far more enduring:

Trust.
Reputation.

Purpose.
Legacy.

I believe entrepreneurs, business leaders, and creators are some of the most influential people in our culture today.

Think about it. We set trends, shape environments, create jobs, and often influence how people live and work.

When we lead with Kingdom principles, reflect Christ in how we serve, lead, and build; we become light in dark places.

That's why this book isn't just another leadership guide. It's a call to arms. A call to stop building side hustles and start building Kingdom hustles.

This book is not about quitting your job or launching a business, though it might lead to that. It's about alignment. Aligning your work with your true assignment.

Each chapter will explore a Kingdom principle of hustle:

Mindset.
Purpose.
Influence.
Discipline.
Rest.
Wealth.
Legacy.

You'll hear from Scripture. You'll get real-world stories.
You'll be challenged to ask hard questions about what you're really building, and who you're building it for.

So, if you've ever felt stuck between your **purpose** and your **paycheck**. If you're tired of working hard and still feeling empty. If you know God has called you to more but you're not sure what that looks like… This book is for you.

Let's stop hustling for crumbs.
Let's start building for the Kingdom.

Let's go.

CHAPTER ONE
The Myth of the Side Hustle

When Exhaustion Becomes Our Badge of Honor.

"You cannot serve both God and money." — *Matthew 6:24*

Sarah's alarm buzzed at 5 a.m., again. Honestly, she wanted to roll over, instead she dragged herself up. Before her family stirred, she was already answering emails for her consulting business, tinkering with her Etsy shop, and sketching out Instagram content. By 6:30 she was flipping pancakes, packing lunches, and nudging kids toward the door. Her "real job" clocked in at 8:30, followed by evening networking events, late night client calls, and weekend market booths.

Sarah liked to call it "living the dream." Her friends said she was inspiring. Her bank account was fuller, her followers were multiplying, and her calendar groaned under the weight of appointments.

So why did she feel so empty? The life she had built looked packed, yet it was hollow at the core.

Sarah's pace isn't unusual. It's practically a cultural template. We live in a world where exhaustion gets worn like a medal and burnout parades as a badge of honor. Hustle is romanticized, side hustles are glorified, and busyness gets equated with value. If your calendar is noisy, your inbox overflowing, and your energy drained, people assume you must be crushing it.

That's the myth. The noisier your life, the more important you seem. The less margin you hold, the more admirable you appear. Underneath that image, though, something quietly unravels.

Even among believers, the pressure that drives the marketplace sneaks into the church. Hustle speak creeps in like a thief. Calling gets reduced to "whatever you do on the side," as if the purpose God planted in you only fits in the leftovers of your week. Many believers build businesses in the margins, not out of strategy but because they're already tangled in commitments that were never God's to begin with.

We've been trained to separate faith from work: ministry on Sunday, business on Monday, rest never. Scripture never drew those lines. Jesus didn't die so we could pencil Him into our schedule; He came to take over the whole page.

When you buy into hustle culture, you trade divine calling for cultural applause. You start measuring success by how many streams of income you juggle instead of how faithfully you steward what God placed in your hands. You become enslaved to momentum, afraid that if you slow down, you'll be left behind.

Here's the Kingdom truth: not every opportunity is a calling. Not every idea is an assignment. Not every hustle is holy. The fuel behind your work often decides whether it builds the Kingdom or burns you out.

What's Fueling Your Hustle?

Every hustle runs on something. For some, it's ambition. For others, fear. Still others are fueled by lack, the desperate drive to prove something, to never feel broke again, to outrun insecurity. The source of your hustle will always shape the fruit of your labor.

If anxiety fuels your work, burnout is guaranteed. If pride drives you, the structure will collapse. When effort is birthed in obedience, it bears fruit in its season. The real question isn't whether you're working hard. It's why.

Motivation matters in the Kingdom. God isn't impressed by effort if it's divorced from His direction. You could grind for all the right reasons in all the wrong ways. You could exhaust yourself and still stand outside His will.

That's why the Word says, *"Acknowledge Him in all your ways, and He will make your paths straight." — Proverbs 3:6.* Not your hustle. His.

When fear builds your business, you'll keep glancing over your shoulder. When comparison builds it, you'll never feel like enough. When it's built on Kingdom vision, peace settles in your soul. You stop chasing the market and start pacing with the Spirit. That pace is actually sustainable.

Misplaced fuel doesn't just drain us. It reshapes our worship.

The False Foundations of Hustle

Idols don't always wear robes and sit on pedestals. Sometimes they wear watches and crouch behind laptops. Hustle, once a servant, morphs into a master. We convince ourselves that more effort means more value, more motion means more meaning. Without noticing, we anchor our identity in doing rather than becoming.

God warned through Ezekiel, *"These men have set up idols in their hearts... Should I let them inquire of me at all?" — Ezekiel 14:3.* That wasn't for pagans. It was for His people. The problem wasn't only their hands. It was their hearts.

When hustle becomes your source of worth, your schedule feels sacred, and surrender seems optional. It often starts innocently, just one more project, one more client, one more late night. Soon, work feels like worship, and burnout gets mistaken for obedience. You're no longer chasing excellence; you're chasing identity.

I tell my kids about consequences, and maybe you do too. It's rarely the sudden crash that takes us out. It's the slow drift. The tiny compromise. The "no big deal" detail. That one overlooked thing matters, because it starts momentum in the wrong direction.

Nobody fears the snowball at first. Left unchecked, it barrels faster than we can stop, and one day we wake up realizing the crash already started.

God won't compete with your idol. If hustle sits on the throne of your heart, He'll shake it until it falls. Not to shame you, but to free you. Sometimes the kindest thing God can do for a Kingdom entrepreneur is to interrupt the idol before it steals the very thing they were born to build.

The Illusion of Self-Made Success

Whether our hustle roots itself in pride or in the illusion of self-made success, the result's the same: our work slides onto a throne that belongs to God alone.

Business history is packed with stories like Howard Schultz of Starbucks. He built one of the most recognized brands on the planet with relentless intensity. Years later, Schultz admitted his obsession nearly cost him his family, his health, and his peace. He built a global empire yet neglected what mattered most, the Kingdom.

You may never run a coffee giant; however, the temptation to build Babel instead of altars creeps into small businesses too. His honesty stands as a caution. Just because the world calls it success doesn't mean Heaven does.

Culture loves the "self-made" label. Kingdom people know better. There's no such thing. Every breath is borrowed. Every opportunity, a gift. Every win, pure grace. When we buy into the lie that we built it all, we cut ourselves off from the Source who sustains it.

"Remember the Lord your God, for it is He who gives you the ability to produce wealth." — Deuteronomy 8:18.

You didn't manufacture your gifting or orchestrate your opportunity. God did. Forget that, and you'll start building Babel instead of altars. You'll swap eternal legacy for temporary clout. You'll gain the world and lose your soul.

Success isn't evil. Unsubmitted success is dangerous.

The Divided Heart

When self-made thinking takes root, hearts fracture. Fractured hearts can't build Kingdom work that lasts. The riskiest part of the side hustle isn't the work. It's the divided heart. Treat your calling like a side project, and you'll treat God like a side note. You'll chase profit over purpose, reach over impact, busyness over obedience. The Kingdom doesn't thrive in fragments. It demands your whole self.

Jesus didn't multitask His way through ministry. He carried one assignment: the will of the Father. That clarity killed distraction. It gave Him freedom to say no, not from laziness, but from focus.

Think of the Proverbs 31 woman. Often misquoted as the ultimate multitasker. Look closer. Every enterprise she managed served one central purpose: stewarding her household and community with wisdom. She wasn't juggling random side gigs; she was building a unified life of impact. Her work showed focus, not fragmentation.

That's the tension every entrepreneur of faith must wrestle with. The world applauds the busiest. Heaven honors the most surrendered.

When you chase your God given assignment with single minded purpose, you begin to see what others miss. You operate with clarity the culture can't replicate. You don't jump at every trend or pivot with every breeze. You build slow, steady, strong. You say yes to God and no to distractions, not once, but daily. In doing so, you anchor your identity in something more eternal than followers or revenue.

What the World Calls Hustle, Heaven Calls Distraction

Here's the trap: distraction feels like devotion when it's dressed as productivity. Hard work isn't the enemy. Jesus worked. Paul worked. Ruth worked. Hustle is more than hard work. It's a mindset of self-dependence. It's urgency that confuses movement with progress. It's believing you can do it all, be it all, have it all, without asking God if He even called you to start.

Heaven doesn't measure by output. It measures by faithfulness.

When Martha was busy hosting, Jesus pointed to Mary, the one at His feet, and said, *"She has chosen what is better, and it will not be taken away from her." — Luke 10:42*.

Mary wasn't lazy. She was present. She was aligned. She was undistracted.

Plenty of believers are sprinting yet missing their moment. They're building platforms God never asked for and chasing influence He never endorsed. The tragedy isn't failing. It's succeeding at the wrong thing.

You can be productive and still miss your purpose; busy and still miss your assignment.

Heaven isn't moved by your schedule. It's stirred by your surrender.

Kingdom Hustle: What It Really Looks Like

If hustle without the Spirit is hollow, what does building with Him look like? Kingdom hustle isn't lazy, yet it's not frantic either. It's not scattered, or ego driven.

It looks like early prayer before the office opens. It looks like hard choices that cost you profit but guard your integrity. It looks like walking away from lucrative deals because the Spirit whispered no. It looks like doing excellent work quietly, because excellence honors God.

That's what Paul meant in Colossians 3:23: *"Whatever you do, work at it with all your heart, as working for the Lord, not for human masters."* That applies not just to pastors but to entrepreneurs, builders, coders, creators, you.

True Kingdom hustle doesn't chase applause. It chases obedience. It may never go viral, yet it will bear fruit.

Think of Lydia in the book of Acts. She was a woman of wealth and influence, known for trading costly purple cloth. When the Gospel reached her through Paul, she didn't abandon her trade. She placed it under new ownership. Her home turned into a gathering place for believers. Her table became an altar. Her business became a conduit for Kingdom impact.

Lydia never separated her faith and work. She wove them together, thread by thread.

The Realignment You Didn't Know You Needed

If business feels heavy, the solution might not be more capacity. It might be recalibration of calling. If you feel tired, anxious, or dissatisfied even as revenue grows, maybe it's not capacity. Maybe it's calling.

You weren't designed to juggle three side hustles and shallow faith. You were designed to walk in step with God, aligned in purpose, committed in heart, faithful in work.

Realignment isn't just a buzzword. It's repentance in motion. It's saying, "Lord, I've built this in my strength. Show me how to rebuild it in Yours." It's shifting focus away from your dreams and centering on His Kingdom.

"Seek first the Kingdom and His righteousness, and all these things will be added to you." — Matthew 6:33.

Not your side hustle. Not your followers. Not your retirement plan. Seek the Kingdom.

This isn't abandoning business. It's surrendering its purpose. You're not giving up productivity. You're redeeming it. Trading chaos for clarity. Moving from endless striving to faithful stewardship.

That kind of shift won't just change your business. It'll change your life.

The Call to Build Differently

Six months after that breaking point, Sarah's alarm still buzzed at 5 a.m. Though, something had changed.

Instead of reaching for her phone, she reached for her Bible. Instead of frantically multitasking before her family woke, she sat in stillness with the One who called her. The consulting business? Still running. The Etsy shop? She closed it. Not out of failure, but out of focus.

Sarah realized she didn't need another strategy to cram more into her day. She needed a Savior to reorder her day completely.

She began asking different questions: "What did God actually call me to build? What am I carrying that He never asked me to pick up?

The shift wasn't instant. It was messy. She disappointed some clients. She walked away from income. She had to explain to well-meaning friends why she was "scaling back" when she'd been "crushing it."

Something remarkable happened. Her revenue didn't collapse. It stabilized. Her family noticed she was present again. Her clients received better work because she wasn't stretched thin. Most importantly, the hollow feeling that had haunted her success began to fill with something she hadn't felt in years: peace.

Sarah stopped hustling to prove her worth. She started building from a place of rest.

Like Sarah, this is your invitation to shift. Not into laziness, but into alignment. Not into passivity, but into purpose.

Hustle isn't evil. Hustle without the Spirit is empty.

You were never meant to build alone. You were meant to co-labor with the God who called you.

Let this chapter be a mirror. Let it poke at your assumptions, confront your ambition, and pull you back to Jesus' feet.

Not because business is bad. Because business without Him is.

You weren't created to hustle to the top. You were created to build something that lasts.

Lay your hustle at His feet. When you do, it won't just be profitable. It'll be eternal.

WALK IT OUT

Living Beyond the Myth

To live beyond the myth, begin by redefining what productivity means in your world. The culture teaches that constant motion equals success, yet the Kingdom calls you to move with intention. Instead of filling every moment with activity, choose assignments that carry eternal value. Ask yourself, "What would still matter if the world stopped watching?" Those are the things worth building. Each morning, invite God into your schedule and ask Him to reveal what truly belongs to this day. Write down what He shows you and hold to it as a sacred blueprint. Everything else can wait.

Establish clear boundaries around your time and guard them like sacred ground. When your workday begins, give it your full focus. When it ends, release it completely. Rest is not a reward; it's a declaration of trust. It says, "God, I believe You're still working when I stop." Treat your boundaries as a form of worship, not restriction. They'll keep your calling from becoming chaos and remind your heart that your worth was never tied to your workload.

As new opportunities appear, pause before you respond. The world celebrates the one who says yes to everything, but Kingdom builders learn to weigh their choices by peace, not pressure. Before committing, whisper a simple prayer: "Lord, is this mine to build?" If peace remains, proceed with confidence. If confusion lingers, wait. Not every open door leads to destiny.

At the close of each day, take a quiet moment to reflect. Ask, "Did I obey what God asked of me today?" Let that be your measure of success. Faithfulness to the assignment always outweighs the number of things completed. Over time, this daily rhythm retrains your heart to see work as partnership rather than performance. You'll notice a new kind of progress; steady, peaceful, deeply purposeful. The myth of the side hustle loses its grip when obedience becomes your pace and presence becomes your power.

CHAPTER TWO
Kingdom Wholeness

The Culture Wants You Busy. The Kingdom Wants You Whole.

"Do not conform to the pattern of this world, but be transformed by the renewing of your mind. Then you will be able to test and approve what God's will is—his good, pleasing and perfect will." — Romans 12:2

We live in a world that worships hustle. From morning motivation reels to late-night strategy sessions, there's always pressure to do more, be more, and produce more. Culture applauds the one who sacrifices sleep, skips meals, and runs on caffeine and anxiety. If you're always grinding, you must be valuable, right?

That's the message, at least. However, here's the truth: culture doesn't care if you burn out, it only cares if you perform. It rewards you for staying late, being always available, and sacrificing family dinners in exchange for online visibility. It offers the illusion of success through more: more streams of income, more engagement, more recognition, more grind. In chasing all this "more," something essential begins to wither: your soul.

Honestly, the Kingdom of God offers something better. God's definition of "more" doesn't always mean addition, it means subtraction: less noise, less striving, less self. The Kingdom invites you into something richer: wholeness. Not just rest, but restoration. Not just slowing down, but being made whole again in body, mind, and spirit. It's not about adding hours to your day, but about aligning your life with God's rhythm.

"Come to me, all you who are weary and burdened, and I will give you rest." — Matthew 11:28

This wasn't a polite suggestion for those who happened to be tired. It was a profound call to anyone exhausted from carrying the weight of self-made identity. Rest, in the Kingdom, isn't a luxury or a sign of laziness; it's obedience. It's an act of trust that says, "God, I believe You are in control even when I stop striving."

When Hustle Becomes a False Gospel

Hustle culture doesn't just drain your energy; it distorts your theology. It teaches that your worth is based on your performance and that success is the ultimate sign of favor. It preaches a gospel of hustle, where your value is earned and your identity is built on output. This is a false gospel. Jesus didn't hand out trophies for burnout.

We don't find Jesus in a hurry. He often walked away from crowds, paused in the middle of urgent situations, and withdrew to pray when His influence was at its highest. Before choosing His twelve disciples He spent the entire night in prayer (*Luke 6:12*). He moved slowly enough to be interrupted, patient enough to pause, and bold enough to say "no" when the crowds wanted more miracles. His pace wasn't dictated by people's demands; it was set by the Father's will.

The story of the woman with the issue of blood in Mark 5 illustrates this. The crowd pressed in, a human sea of demand and noise. Jesus was on His way to heal Jairus' daughter, a high-stakes, urgent situation by any measure. The culture of that moment would have demanded He move swiftly, prioritizing the important person and the obvious need. However, when this woman, a social outcast, dared to touch the hem of His garment, Jesus stopped. He didn't condemn or deny her because she was breaking the purity regulation. No; he stopped the entire operation to look at this one person, acknowledge her faith, and restore her dignity.

Jesus wasn't just healing her body; He was affirming her worth.

This intentional pause in the midst of chaos is a message in itself: people matter more than the agenda, and presence outweighs performance. It's a powerful response to the idea that we must rush past the individual to serve the crowd.

Contrast that with modern expectations. In a recent Deloitte survey, 77% of employees reported experiencing burnout in their current roles. Entrepreneurs often feel it even more intensely, driven by the pressure to perform, stay visible, and produce outcomes daily. The result is an epidemic of exhaustion masquerading as success.

In the Kingdom, fruitfulness flows from abiding, not striving. Jesus declared, *"I am the vine; you are the branches. If you remain in me and I in you, you will bear much fruit; apart from me you can do nothing."* —*John 15:5*.

This isn't poetic suggestion; it's a framework for life and leadership. When you start from rest, instead of racing toward it, you tap into a power that doesn't deplete but renews.

You Were Made for a Different Rhythm

Culture is fast, loud, and reactionary. It demands instant results and fears obscurity. It breeds anxiety by linking your worth to your output. It's like living inside a ticking clock, loud, urgent, and always counting down. However, the Kingdom is steady. It honors the hidden work, trusts the unseen process, and is unbothered by delayed recognition.

There's no scarcity in Heaven. There's no rush to beat the algorithm, no need to outperform the competition. In God's economy, success is not a race, it's a relationship. Maybe that's why this rhythm isn't an exotic practice reserved for monks; it's woven into the fabric of a faithful life. It's the intentional pause before opening your inbox, a moment to pray before the day's demands begin. It's the Sabbath rest that shuts off your phone, not just to recharge, but to declare God's sovereignty. It's the courage to walk away from a deal that compromises your peace, even at a loss of significant profit.

This is how we begin to live out our theology. The Kingdom's pace honors the hidden work of prayer, the quiet process of character formation, and the slow, steady faithfulness that culture often overlooks. It's a pace that allows us to be present and to trust that God is at work, even when the results are not immediately visible.

The Apostle Paul warned believers in Rome not to conform to the culture around them. That transformation isn't a one-time event; it's a daily refusal to be discipled by the world's systems.

Real transformation begins when you stop measuring your life by cultural metrics: money, popularity, speed, and start aligning with the eternal markers of obedience, faithfulness, and trust.

Culture Says Compete. The Kingdom Says Collaborate

One of the most destructive side effects of hustle culture is the constant comparison it creates. There's always someone ahead of you, someone younger, richer, more charismatic, more "successful." Culture turns success into a scoreboard, where someone else's win means your loss. The Kingdom doesn't operate on scarcity. When one wins, we all win. When one suffers, we all grieve. As Paul writes, *"Now you are the body of Christ, and each one of you is a part of it."* — *1 Corinthians 12:27*.

You're not in competition with other Kingdom builders; you're in covenant with them. Covenant over competition changes how we lead, serve, and build. It makes room for celebration without insecurity and generosity without fear. As former president, JFK, said often, "a rising tide lifts all boats."

If you look around and take an inventory, you'll notice that in every industry there is plenty of room for growth. That means there's plenty of room for opportunity. Plenty of room to collaborate and feed off each other's successes rather than running hoarding every lead, every answer, or every system. This doesn't mean you must give away all of your specifics, but it means you should trust God's design for us all to be united in mind and action.

I know of two Kingdom builders who run similar marketing agencies. By all worldly measures, they should be fierce competitors, clawing for the same clients, resources, and recognition. Yet, they meet regularly to share best practices, send clients to each other when one is a better fit, and actively pray for one another's success.

Their covenant has led to mutual abundance, proving that the pie doesn't have to be sliced; it can be multiplied. This is what it looks like to live out the truth that we're all part of the same body.

This also reshapes how you build. You're not marketing to impress; you're ministering to impact. You're not hustling to prove; you're stewarding what God entrusted. That's a completely different posture, and one that brings peace.

Redefining Success

Let's face it, culture keeps moving the goalposts. Today it's followers, tomorrow it's revenue, next week it's reach, then it's AI-driven innovation. If you chase these things as your source of identity, you'll never rest, because there's always someone ahead. However, when God is the One measuring, you don't have to run faster, you just have to be faithful.

Success in the Kingdom isn't defined by speed or scale, but by surrender. The scoreboard of Heaven is often flipped from the scoreboard of the world. Noah looked like a failure until it started to rain. Joseph's faithfulness in prison didn't look impressive until the palace door opened. For years, all anyone saw was a dreamer, a slave, and then a prisoner. Still, God was building him for a purpose greater than his comfort.

Jesus Himself looked like a public failure on Friday, but Heaven flipped the scoreboard on Sunday. His apparent defeat was the very victory the world needed. Obedience often looks like losing, until Heaven calls it victory. This reorientation of success is crucial for anyone building in God's economy.

I have a close friend who decided that his business wasn't to benefit himself, but to benefit the Kingdom. He changed the culture and attitude, and along the way God richly blessed him more than ever. When his priorities shifted from hustle to stewardship, the success didn't disappear, it deepened. That's the Kingdom in action.

Your job isn't to chase results, it's to stay obedient. Let God take care of the outcomes.

Letting Go of Cultural Control

One of the great temptations in business and life is to try and control every outcome. If we can plan better, optimize more, and hustle harder, we believe we can make success inevitable. However, Kingdom work requires open hands.

Faith doesn't mean you abandon strategy. It means you don't worship it. God may call you to build something that doesn't scale fast. He may lead you down a path that feels inefficient to the world but is effective in Heaven. Think of Abraham, who left his home without knowing his destination; or David, anointed as king but sent back to the fields. God's timeline almost always disrupts our expectations.

The culture clings. The Kingdom releases. The more tightly you grip your plans, the harder it is to hold God's promises.

You Are a Living Rebuttal

Every time you choose peace over panic, truth over trend, rest over striving, you're preaching. Your life becomes a living sermon. Your business becomes a witness.

The world doesn't need more Christian-theme d branding. It needs more Christ-shaped builders. Entrepreneurs who carry the presence of God into meetings, marketing strategies, and client calls. Those who set prices with integrity, treat people with dignity, and let the fruit of the Spirit guide their decisions.

This kind of life can't be copied, it must be cultivated, and when people see it, they notice something different. They feel the weight of Heaven in the way you work.

Kingdom Culture Is a Different Kind of Success

Building in the Kingdom doesn't mean you won't work hard. It means your work is anchored in a different why. Your results matter, but not more than your relationships. Your goals matter, but not more than God's guidance.

When you align your pace with the Prince of Peace, you don't just avoid burnout, you invite breakthrough. You become a builder of something eternal. Not trendy. Not shallow, but lasting. Legacy-worthy.

That's the invitation: to move at the speed of grace. To trade cultural pressure for Kingdom presence. To build from rest, not for it. Because you're not here to mimic culture, you're here to reform it. You're not just a Christian in business; you're a Kingdom ambassador. A builder of what this world can't manufacture, because what you carry was authored in Heaven.

This truth is not a theological theory meant only for the church; it's a marketplace mandate with tangible, real-world results. This is exactly what happened when two engineers named Bill Hewlett and Dave Packard founded their technology company in a Palo Alto garage. I once heard a leader at the company, which grew to become the global giant Hewlett-Packard (HP)™, describe the culture this way: "Our business isn't an engine for profit; it's a greenhouse for people."

This vision shifted everything. From the beginning, the founders intentionally chose to prioritize integrity over expediency, rest over rush, and community over competition, principles now famously known as The HP Way.

Instead of focusing solely on the bottom line, their foundational philosophy focused on respect for employees, trust, and decentralization. Years later, their company isn't just known for its excellent, innovative products and status as one of the largest computer manufacturing and sales businesses in the world. It's known for launching leaders, pioneering the Silicon Valley culture, and maintaining an enduring legacy that spanned decades. The fruit of their wholeness, their commitment to these Kingdom-aligned values, was a culture of multiplication. What they built wasn't just a business, but a legacy. It proved that moving with intention, rather than just raw ambition, is the most sustainable path to growth.

So, breathe. Slow down. Start listening again.

Let the culture chase busy.

You? You're here to be whole.

WALK IT OUT

The Rhythm of Enough

To live within the rhythm of enough, you must first believe that peace is productive. The world measures success by how much you can accomplish, yet heaven measures it by how deeply you can trust. Begin each day by acknowledging that your limits aren't weaknesses; they're part of God's design. When you accept that you're not meant to do everything, you finally make space for Him to move in what you can't control.

Set a clear beginning and ending to your workday and honor them as acts of obedience. When you close your laptop or lock your tools away, resist the urge to return "just to finish one more thing." Choose to end your day knowing that God finishes what you leave in His hands. Your boundaries protect what your busyness tries to steal: rest, relationships, and renewal. Over time, those boundaries teach you that blessing doesn't come from burnout; it comes from balance.

Throughout the day, practice moments of pause. Take ten quiet minutes where you do nothing but breathe, listen, and thank God for the breath that sustains you. These pauses recalibrate your soul. They remind you that life is more than work and that your identity isn't found in constant movement. The stillness you make room for today becomes the strength you carry tomorrow.

At the close of each evening, define what "enough" truly meant for that day. Ask, "Did I honor what God asked of me, or did I chase what culture told me mattered?" Then release the rest to Him. This daily habit transforms pressure into peace and striving into steadiness. In time, you'll discover that the rhythm of enough isn't about slowing down; it's about walking in step with God's provision, confident that what He gives is always sufficient for what He's called you to build.

CHAPTER THREE
Work Was God's First Assignment

Created to Work with God.

"The Lord God took the man and put him in the Garden of Eden to work it and take care of it." — Genesis 2:15

If culture demands performance, the Kingdom invites purpose. From the very beginning, that purpose was grounded in work. Before sin entered the world, before brokenness, pain, or even the first act of worship, there was labor.

God placed Adam in Eden not to relax, but to *"work it and take care of it."* This was humanity's first assignment. Not rest. Not leisure. Not even ministry. Work. Work wasn't a punishment. It was design.

In a perfect, unfallen world, God entrusted responsibility to humanity. From the beginning, work was sacred, an invitation to co-labor with God in cultivating what He created. God, the ultimate worker, spent six days creating a world of order, purpose, and beauty. On the seventh day, He rested. He then placed Adam into the magnificent creation to continue the work: to name the animals, to tend the land, and to bring forth the potential of a flourishing world. He wasn't just a gardener; he was sub-creator, an image-bearer reflecting the very nature of his God.

That truth has been buried beneath centuries of distortion. Today, work is often seen as a necessary evil, something to endure until retirement, financial independence, or vocational escape. Even within Christian culture, a false hierarchy elevates ministry above the marketplace, making business leaders, craftsmen, and entrepreneurs feel spiritually second-rate. This divide between sacred and secular work has no place in Scripture. According to God's original blueprint, all meaningful work, when aligned with

His will, is spiritual.

Work as Worship

In *Genesis*, there was no divide between Adam's labor and his relationship with God. The Garden was both a sanctuary and a workplace. Adam didn't clock in and out of spiritual moments. He walked with God while naming animals and tending the land. There were no pulpits, microphones, or church services; there was only presence and purpose, intertwined.

This ancient truth stands in stark contrast to how we often live today. We limit God's presence to sanctuaries and Sunday services. In Eden, His presence was found in the soil, in the sweat, and in the stewardship. The Garden wasn't sacred because it was quiet; it was sacred because it was aligned. The rhythm of work and worship wasn't separate; it was the same.

"Whatever you do, work at it with all your heart, as working for the Lord, not for human masters." — Colossians 3:23

Paul wasn't offering empty encouragement or productivity advice. He was reframing the very nature of work. *"Whatever you do"* means exactly that: every email, every sales call, every job site, every spreadsheet, every service appointment. When you're buried under QuickBooks tabs and calls that don't stop, it's easy to forget the sacred in the struggle. However, when done with the posture of worship, even the most mundane tasks become sacred offerings.

The Hebrew word for *"work"* in *Genesis 2:15* is ʻ*ābad*, a word that also means *"worship"* or *"serve."* That overlap is intentional. In God's language, labor and liturgy go hand in hand. The most powerful work you can do is an act of worship. Worship isn't confined to music or sermons; it's how we serve, how we show up, and how we steward what has been entrusted to us.

Of course, this is easier said than done. When you're buried under deadlines, stuck in traffic, or answering your fiftieth email before lunch, it's easy to lose the sacred in the cycle. Kingdom perspective doesn't hinge on how spiritual something feels; it hinges on whom it's offered to. Worship isn't about emotion; it's about intention. When you invite God into your work, your desk becomes an altar, and your tasks become offerings.

You don't need a title to serve. You don't need a stage to preach. All you need is a surrendered heart, willing hands, and the conviction that wherever you work, God is with you.

Work vs. Toil

It's important to realize that work existed before the curse. Sin didn't create labor; it created toil. After the fall, God told Adam:

"Cursed is the ground because of you; through painful toil you will eat food from it all the days of your life." — Genesis 3:17

The curse affected the environment of work, not the calling itself. The ground became resistant. Weeds and thorns began to choke out the crops. What was once joyful and collaborative became strained and resistant, but the assignment didn't change. Work wasn't revoked; it was redefined.

Author and speaker, Jim Rohn, often reminded his audiences that if you neglect your field, weeds take over. He would say that discipline weighs ounces but regret weighs tons. His wisdom echoes Eden. Adam was placed in the garden not to avoid responsibility, but to tend it faithfully. Work isn't a curse; it's cultivation. The fruit of labor comes when we show up with diligence.

Ignore the field and thorns appear. Cultivate it and abundance follows. The principle hasn't changed. From Adam's soil to our spreadsheets, stewardship determines the harvest.

That distinction matters because it reframes our understanding of labor. Work isn't simply a means of survival. It's a core part of your identity as an image-bearer of a working God. When we forget that, we begin to resent what God designed to refine us. That's when dissatisfaction creeps in. Often, the problem isn't the work; it's the absence of purpose behind it.

You Were Made to Build

God is not only our Redeemer; He's also our Creator. The *Genesis* narrative portrays Him as an architect, designer, and craftsman. He brings order to chaos, speaks light into darkness, and breathes life into dust. Then He hands that creative baton to us.

The human drive to design, develop, solve, and build isn't a product of ambition gone wild; it's the fingerprint of the God. When you lead with integrity, build systems that bless others, or bring beauty into your field, you reflect God's character.

Good work feeds more than your bank account; it feeds your purpose, because it aligns with how you were made. However, when you remove God from your work, that same drive becomes distortion. You start hustling for identity, chasing approval, and measuring your worth by your output. Work becomes something we endure, not embody. That isn't Kingdom. That's culture.

The Gospel in Your Work

In a broken world, your work becomes a powerful stage for the Gospel. It's not just about what you produce; it's about how you embody the truth of Christ in a workplace marked by the effects of the Fall.

The world sees burnout, greed, and ruthless competition. When you operate with a Kingdom perspective, you can bring light into dark places. Your work can become a tangible expression of redemption. A business owner who prioritizes people over profit models the heart of the Good Shepherd. A team member who acts with integrity in a cutthroat environment reveals the righteousness of God. A leader who practices forgiveness and grace when an employee fails demonstrates the love of Christ.

Your work isn't a distraction from the Gospel; it's a vehicle for it. The good work you do, expressed through excellence, integrity, and servant leadership, becomes a testament to the transformative power of a life redeemed by grace.

Work as Witness

Truett Cathy, founder of Chick-fil-A, knew that work could be worship. When others told him staying closed on Sundays would cripple revenue, he didn't waver. Honoring God came first.

"I wasn't so committed to financial success that I was willing to abandon my principles and priorities," he said. That decision, in a purely financial sense, cost the company millions. Spiritually, it became a signpost. Cathy built more than a restaurant; he built with conviction. That conviction multiplied not only profits, but influence.

Today, Chick-fil-A leads the industry in per-location revenue. Its legacy isn't merely economic; it's spiritual. Cathy proved that business can be discipleship. Work, when Kingdom-aligned, becomes witness.

Work Shapes Character

God doesn't just use work to accomplish things; He uses it to transform people. Labor is one of His most consistent tools for spiritual formation. It teaches perseverance when plans fall apart. It humbles us when others outperform us. It forces us to navigate tension, take responsibility, and confront our limits. Work is where true growth happens.

You might study patience in a sermon, but you embody it under pressure. You can learn about forgiveness in Scripture, but you practice it with a difficult coworker. Promotions reveal pride. Layoffs reveal dependence. In both, God is asking a searching question: Do you trust Me more than your title? Whether you're climbing the ladder or picking up the pieces, His goal isn't your status; it's your surrender.

"Lazy hands make for poverty, but diligent hands bring wealth." — Proverbs 10:4

Excellence isn't just about results; it's about reverence. How you work reveals how you worship. When you honor your calling, you honor God. That's why God cares how we build, not just what we build. In the process of building with Him, we become more like Him.

Work with Calling

Florence Nightingale, the founder of modern nursing, didn't separate her faith from her field. Born into privilege in Victorian England, she felt called to serve the sick. That call cost her societal favor and personal comfort, but she obeyed.

During the Crimean War, she revolutionized battlefield hygiene and drastically reduced mortality rates. Her work was unglamorous and grueling. Yet she once wrote, *"I can offer Him nothing except work."* That line says everything. She didn't see her job as separate from her worship. For her, it was worship.

Her legacy reshaped an industry. More importantly, her life was aligned. When your work and your worship align, the impact stretches far beyond your field.

Your Work Is a Platform

"Let your light shine before others, that they may see your good deeds and glorify your Father in heaven." — Matthew 5:16

Your business, your leadership, your craft, and your service are Kingdom territory. Every email, every meeting, and every decision is a stage. Your daily excellence is a sermon. You don't need to quote scripture to witness. When your contracts are honest, your culture is kind, and your delivery exceeds expectations, you're preaching Him without words.

There's a difference between doing work for God and doing work with God. Working for Him can become striving. Working with Him brings surrender.

One exhausts. The other empowers.

When you work with God, you invite His presence into the process. Meetings carry peace. Projects reflect purpose. Your job becomes an altar. Your life becomes a testimony. Your faith becomes visible, not because you're loud, but because you're faithful.

That faithfulness becomes a beacon, pointing people not just to a better Kingdom, but to the King Himself.

The State Trooper's Platform

When I was five, my seven-year-old sister and I were in the car with a family friend who had been drinking. A state trooper pulled him over and subsequently arrested him for drunk driving.

After the situation was handled, the trooper approached us; my sister and I. We were terrified. We never experienced a situation like that. Little did we know, the trooper wasn't there to simply enforce the law; he was there on a divine assignment.

When the trooper stood in front of us, he reached out his hand and gave my sister and I a pack of Reese's Pieces™. To us, in that moment, it was just candy. However, later in life I realized it was so much more. That small gesture was meant to calm our fears and reclaim a sliver of kindness from a deeply negative situation.

I carry that memory and that feeling with me to this day. I don't recall his name or his age, but I recall his generosity and kindness. Today, I carry that same kindness and mindset into all my interactions.

A small gesture from a faithful public servant reshaped my future in ways he'll never know. His impact has paid dividends he may never see until he reaches Heaven.

That's the power of a platform repurposed for the Kingdom.

WALK IT OUT

Working With Worship

To work with worship means to see every task as sacred, no matter how routine it feels. Begin each day by dedicating your work to God in prayer. Invite His presence into what you build, manage, or repair. Whisper a simple acknowledgment that your effort belongs to Him. When you remember that the work itself is an altar, even ordinary moments begin to glow with purpose. Excellence stops being about reputation and starts becoming about reverence.

Keep your focus on stewardship rather than status. When you treat your job, craft, or business as something entrusted to you, everything shifts. Excellence becomes your offering. Integrity becomes your language of praise. Do what's right even when no one notices, because you understand that heaven always sees. Over time, your diligence will speak louder than any title.

Carry gratitude into every part of your labor. Thank God for the ability to think, to move, to create. Gratitude turns frustration into fuel and transforms deadlines into opportunities for devotion. When you encounter difficulty, pause long enough to ask, "Lord, what are You teaching me through this?" That simple question can turn pressure into presence.

At the end of each day, reflect on the work of your hands. Ask whether it reflected His heart. If it did, rest in that. If it didn't, bring it before Him and begin again tomorrow. Working with worship isn't about perfection; it's about posture. It's choosing to see God in the details and to make excellence a hymn of honor. When you work this way, your labor becomes love in motion, and every day becomes a chance to glorify the One who gave you the ability to build.

CHAPTER FOUR
The King's Assignment

Created for a Purpose. Sent on Assignment.

"For we are God's handiwork, created in Christ Jesus to do good works, which God prepared in advance for us to do." — Ephesians 2:10

What if your job title isn't your real title? What if Heaven calls you something no business card ever will?

Your story didn't begin in a hospital room; it began in the heart of God. Before you inhaled your first breath, Heaven had already whispered your name. Long before you ever wondered about your purpose, your Creator had written one.

You were formed by design, for a reason, by a King who gives His people assignments: not hobbies, not filler work, and certainly not aimless wandering. Assignment is identity in motion.

Scripture echoes this truth across generations. Moses wasn't spared from infanticide by chance. Hidden in a basket, raised in a palace, and exiled to a desert, none of it was wasted. Each season prepared him for a burning bush that would define his calling. Esther didn't win a beauty contest; she was positioned to stand in the gap for a nation. Jeremiah, young and hesitant, still heard God say: *"Before I formed you in the womb I knew you, before you were born I set you apart."* —Jeremiah 1:5

These stories, and yours, reveal a pattern. God does not create without commissioning. Whether you build homes, raise children, lead companies, care for patients, or mentor the forgotten, your life is not random. You weren't born to invent your identity. You were born to discover your assignment. This is the profound truth of *Ephesians 2:10*: your life is not a blank canvas you must fill, but a masterpiece you must unveil.

You Weren't Born to Wing It

Many people drift through life treating purpose like a scavenger hunt. They jump from job to job, hobby to hobby, hoping fulfillment will magically appear, but God's design for you is not accidental. You were not created to improvise your way through existence; you were born with a mission etched into your soul. The burdens that grip your heart, the injustices that keep you awake at night, and the passions that will not let go are often clues to your calling.

Just about everyone today is familiar with Dave Ramsey. Not everyone knows how his journey began. Through a personal financial crisis God led him to start offering biblical, common-sense advice on a single radio station in Nashville.

In the early days, his radio show was unpaid, but he used the platform to promote his self-published book, Financial Peace™, which he sold directly from the trunk of his car. The book's success demonstrated the high demand for his practical guidance, and the show grew in popularity, eventually becoming a nationally syndicated program.

Today, what started as a small, local effort has transformed into Ramsey Solutions, a large company with over 1,000 team members, annual revenues above a half billion dollars, a corporate headquarters in Franklin, Tennessee, and a diverse range of financial products and services, including live events, books, and digital tools like the EveryDollar™ budgeting app. The company's mission remains the same: to provide hope and education to people seeking to change their financial lives.

Maybe your burden is closer to home. Perhaps it's the silent ache of single mothers in your city, the foster care system you can't ignore, or the spiritual apathy you notice in your workplace. These aren't random feelings; they're divine invitations. When you feel a weight for something, it's often God's way of calling you to be part of the solution.

It may not look spectacular. It may look like quiet consistency: praying in secret, working with integrity when no one notices, or showing up faithfully in places that feel invisible. What is unseen by the world is never unseen by God.

God wired you with holy intent. As Frederick Buechner once said: "The place God calls you to is the place where your deep gladness and the world's deep hunger meet."

That intersection is where your assignment lives.

Culture vs. Kingdom

We live in a culture obsessed with identity discovery. There are endless personality tests, guided meditations, self-help seminars, and morning rituals, all designed to help you "find yourself." The message is clear: look inward long enough, and purpose will eventually rise to the surface.

Jesus, however, never told His disciples to *"look within."* He told them to follow Him. Peter wasn't called to analyze himself; he was called to leave his boat. Paul didn't discover his destiny through journaling or vision-casting; he was struck blind, brought to his knees, and told to surrender.

Dietrich Bonhoeffer said it plainly: "When Christ calls a man, He bids him come and die."

The journey of calling is not one of self-enhancement but of self-abandonment. Culture says, "Become who you want to be," while the Kingdom says, "Become who He created you to be." Transformation doesn't happen in isolation; it happens in proximity. Purpose is revealed not by looking inward, but by walking closely with the One who made you. In losing your life for His sake, you truly find it, and in dying to your own desires, you are resurrected into His purpose. This is the difference between a life of constant searching and a life of profound surrender.

Assignment Before Ambition

Ambition is a good servant but a terrible master.

Ambition isn't inherently wrong, but in the Kingdom, it must be surrendered. Ambition without assignment becomes dangerous, leading us into striving, insecurity, and even disobedience.

David wasn't looking for a crown. He was protecting sheep, writing psalms, and fighting off lions when no one was watching. God called him because of his heart, not his résumé. His anointing as king was a private affair, sealed in a field, not broadcast on a stage. Saul, on the other hand, had the throne but not the humility. His unchecked ambition, born from a desire to please men instead of God, cost him everything.

Joseph dreamed of leadership, but God shaped him through betrayal, false accusations, and prison. Each trial refined him, and each setback was a stage of formation, not punishment. His influence came not because he fought for a platform, but because he proved faithful in hidden places. He didn't build a name for himself; he faithfully stewarded the assignment given to him in the pit, in Potiphar's house, and in the prison.

Even Jesus submitted to obscurity, with thirty years of anonymity preceding three years of ministry. He didn't grasp for opportunity; He waited for the Father's timing.

Ambition becomes holy when it kneels before assignment. When ambition leads, it corrupts. When assignment leads, it clarifies.

Discerning Your Kingdom Assignment

When ambition bows to assignment, we become more sensitive to the voice of God. How, then, do we discern what He is truly asking of us?

Start with your burden. What breaks your heart? What do you see that others don't? Nehemiah didn't apply to rebuild Jerusalem; he wept over it. His tears became his blueprint, and his burden became the signpost of his assignment.

Next, examine your gifting. What flows naturally through you and builds others up? Don't confuse applause-worthy skills with altar-worthy gifts. The former draws crowds: the latter builds the Kingdom. Your gifts are the tools God has given you to execute your assignment.

Finally, pay attention to opportunity. Where has God opened unexpected doors? What conversations, relationships, or moments of favor keep showing up? These are the signposts of His divine timing and provision.

Where burden, gifting, and opportunity intersect, that is where assignment lives.

Calling is the why: to glorify God and serve His Kingdom. Assignment is the where: the specific context in which you serve. Gifting is the how: the unique way you're wired to carry it out.

The closer you walk with the King, the clearer your assignment becomes.

When the Map Isn't Given

Most of us want clarity before obedience. We want five-year plans, high-resolution roadmaps, and assurance that our steps will lead somewhere meaningful; however, in the Kingdom of God, clarity often follows obedience, not the other way around.

When God called Abraham, He didn't give him a destination. He simply said: *"Go from your country... to the land I will show you."* — Genesis 12:1

Abraham didn't need to know where; he needed to know who was leading. This is a profound model for every Kingdom leader. Our human minds crave the map, but God offers the Guide.

God rarely gives full instructions. He gives invitations to follow, trust, and move. While we long for control, He asks for surrender. While we seek direction, He offers presence. It's in that presence that we find the courage to keep walking when the way is unclear.

"Whether you turn to the right or to the left, your ears will hear a voice behind you saying, 'This is the way; walk in it.'" — Isaiah 30:21

God doesn't hand us the map in advance. He becomes the guide in the moment.

The Vehicle Is Not the Assignment

One of the most common traps in calling is confusing the vehicle with the assignment. Your job, role, title, or ministry is not your mission; it's simply the current way your mission travels.

Jesus was a carpenter, then a rabbi, then a suffering servant. The roles shifted, but the mission never did: to redeem the lost and reveal the heart of the Father.

In your life, the same pattern holds. You may influence many in one season and mentor one in the next. Your platform may grow or shrink, but your assignment does not expire when your role changes; it only deepens.

I once thought I was simply a construction business owner until a conversation reframed everything. I was listening to one of my favorite comedians, Michael Jr., when he said something that completely shifted my perspective on calling.

In his special More Than Funny, Michael Jr. shared a moment where he redefined the purpose behind his craft. He said he used to focus on getting laughs from the audience, on receiving. He then had a mindset shift: instead of trying to get people to laugh, he began to give them the gift of laughter.

It may sound like a small change, but it's everything. One approach is driven by need, the other by purpose. He illustrated the shift with a simple but powerful example: "If you're a mechanic, you might think you get paid to fix cars, but with this mindset shift, you're really helping people reach their desired destination."

That insight hit me deeply. It reframed everything. I realized I wasn't just running a small construction company; I was leading a team of men, and I had an opportunity to reflect Christ to them in ways most business owners never do. I wasn't simply fixing houses. I was helping homeowners steward and protect one of their most valuable earthly possessions. That moment turned my work into a mission. What once felt ordinary now felt sacred.

When the method shifts, do not panic. The mission remains.

The Assignment Shapes the Worker

It's easy to believe you've missed your moment. Others seem so far ahead, building platforms, launching ministries, and doing what you thought you'd be doing by now. God's timing, however, rarely aligns with our expectations.

Moses was called at eighty.

Jesus waited thirty years.

Paul spent years in silence before leading anything.

The delay was not wasted; it was formative.

Seasons of delay are holy ground. God uses them to shape what public platforms can't. That's where He grows dependence, purifies motives, and prepares you for what's next. The public anointing is often a direct result of the private preparation. You're not behind; you're being built.

We often expect calling to feel extraordinary. The Kingdom, however, moves through the ordinary and mundane.

Ruth gleaned in fields. Joseph stewarded a prison. A boy offered his lunch. These are small moments with eternal impact.

You may never see the full scope of your obedience this side of heaven; Heaven still sees it. Every spreadsheet completed in faith, every diaper changed in love, every quiet act of service; it all counts.

In the Kingdom, the mundane is often the medium for the miraculous. Calling is not for the few; it's for the faithful. Jesus didn't build a fortress and wait for the world to come to Him. He sent His followers out into the broken, the busy, and the overlooked. He still sends today.

Your job title may say teacher, manager, or barista. Your real title, however, is disciple. God isn't just using you to do something; He's using your assignment as a way to transform you.

Of course, not everyone responds. Judas Iscariot walked with Jesus, heard every teaching, saw every miracle, and still sold Him for silver. The rich young ruler had an invitation to follow, but the price was too high.

Assignment is a gift, but it still requires a yes.

The Watchmaker's Assignment

Corrie ten Boom was a watchmaker in a small, family-run watch shop in Haarlem, Netherlands. During World War II, however, the King gave her a new assignment: to hide Jews from the Nazis. Her family's watch shop, which was a public vehicle for their trade, became a secret vehicle for God's mission. The tools she had mastered in her craft: precision, attention to detail, and a deep understanding of small, intricate parts were the very gifts God used to build a secret room in her house.

Her role as a watchmaker was a quiet, faithful obedience that prepared her for a public, life-or-death mission. She didn't abandon her trade. She repurposed it for the Kingdom, a testament to the truth that our assignment is often hidden within the very ordinary skills and roles we already have.

Lasting Words

There is no universal path to purpose, no one-size-fits-all template. Your assignment is handcrafted, unique, and unfolding. At times it may be fast or slow, clear or confusing, but it's always intentional. Stay near to Jesus, following when He speaks and trusting when He is silent, for faith is your foundation, intimacy is your strategy, and obedience is your blueprint.

You weren't made for comfort. You were made for calling.

So, ask again, with fresh ears and a willing heart: What's the assignment within the job I already have? Where have I let fear of man silence my obedience to God? What will I stop doing to make room for what God is building?

When He speaks, don't wait until you feel "ready." Move, because the world is waiting for what God placed inside you.

WALK IT OUT

Hearing And Holding the Assignment

To hear and hold your assignment is to live with spiritual clarity and steady focus. God doesn't hide His will from His builders; He reveals it to those who are still enough to listen. Begin by creating intentional moments of quiet where you can hear His direction without distraction. Before you start your day, silence the noise and ask, "Lord, what are You asking of me in this season?" Write what He brings to mind, even if it seems small. That single act of obedience often unlocks your next step.

Once you've heard His instruction, hold it close. The world will offer shortcuts, louder voices, and competing paths, but faithfulness will always bear more fruit than frenzy. Guard your calling the way a farmer guards seed. Protect it from comparison, fear, and overcommitment. You don't need to understand the entire plan to trust the One who gave it. Focus on the portion He's assigned to you today and do it with excellence.

Surround yourself with people who remind you of what God said when you're tempted to forget. The right voices bring accountability and alignment. When discouragement rises, return to your notes, your journal, or your prayer list. Revisit what God first spoke. His instructions don't expire simply because time has passed.

Holding your assignment also means walking with humility. Stay teachable, stay prayerful, and resist the urge to rush ahead of God's timing. The same God who gave you the vision will provide the provision when it's needed. Your job is not to make it happen but to remain faithful while He does.

Each day you choose obedience over impulse, you strengthen the foundation of your purpose. Over time, that quiet faithfulness will tell the story of a life that listened well, carried what was entrusted, and finished what heaven began.

CHAPTER FIVE
Vision Over Virality

Build What Lasts, Not What Trends.

"So we fix our eyes not on what is seen, but on what is unseen, since what is seen is temporary, but what is unseen is eternal." — 2 Corinthians 4:18

Do you ever feel that tug to go viral? To be seen, trending, keeping pace with a world spinning at breakneck speed. These days, clicks are treated like currency, and fleeting fame often overshadows true impact. Honestly, it can feel suffocating. So, how do we know the difference between genuine purpose and the blaring call of the spotlight?

While culture builds wide, the Kingdom builds deep.

God gives assignments, not suggestions, and His assignments are never about speed; they're about substance. If you want to walk in your calling with clarity and power, you need more than ambition or applause. You need vision, God-breathed vision. The kind that anchors your soul when the spotlight fades and the world scrolls on without you.

Here's the truth that few will say out loud: virality doesn't equal validity. Going viral isn't the same as walking in victory. Just because a crowd is watching doesn't mean God is blessing. Some of the most celebrated spiritual influencers have crashed hard, not because their platforms were inherently evil, but because the platform outpaced the foundation.

The Kingdom doesn't measure success by reach. It measures success by obedience.

The Trap of Trending

Culture lures entrepreneurs and leaders with the glittering promise of influence. Algorithms reward immediacy. Headlines reward controversy. Attention itself has become a kind of intoxicating currency, sometimes even more addictive than money.

In a world where virality equals value, the pressure to stay visible never lets up. It's not enough to be excellent; you must also be loud. It's not enough to be consistent; you must be sensational. Flash takes priority over faithfulness. Performance overshadows purpose.

The Kingdom doesn't play by those rules. God doesn't build for clicks. He builds for character. Character usually gets forged in hidden places, quiet spaces, away from applause, where culture isn't watching. That's why the chase for virality is such a dangerous trap. It feeds comparison. It sparks envy. It creates a constant hum of anxiety, because the metric of success is always external and always shifting. When your worth hangs on numbers on a screen, you hand over your peace and trade authenticity for approval. Before long, you become a prisoner to the very audience you thought you were leading. It's a modern form of digital idolatry.

Sometimes, vision requires you to say no to the very thing the world says will make you successful. Saying yes to one thing is always saying no to something else. Vision demands exclusivity. Each time you commit to a direction, you're simultaneously closing the door to countless others. Some doors close to guard your focus. Others close because you traded opportunity for distraction. You can't say yes to Kingdom vision and yes to everything the world waves in front of you.

A builder who constantly shifts blueprints never finishes the house. When you chase every trend, you dilute your focus. When you try to please everyone, you dilute your obedience.

If your yes is going to matter, it must cost you a few strategic no's. A vision that comes from God will require the discipline to ignore what feels urgent so you can pursue what's eternal.

We're not here to trend. We're here to transform.

To truly build for eternity, we must look beyond the fleeting metrics of modern influence and learn from those who built according to Heaven's blueprint, not worldly hype.

Heaven Moves on Vision, Not Hype

Biblical history is full of visionaries who were never celebrated in their time. They weren't invited to speak at conferences. They didn't have brand deals or blue checks. They didn't ride waves of popularity or cater to public opinion. They were often rejected, mocked, and isolated. Yet they walked in vision, and because of that, they changed everything.

Noah built for over a century without a single follower. Imagine it: hammering away at a giant boat in a land that had never seen rain, explaining a vision no one could grasp. He wasn't trending; he was trusting. *"By faith Noah, when warned about things not yet seen, in holy fear built an ark to save his family."* — Hebrews 11:7

His faith made no sense to the world, but it made history in Heaven.

Nehemiah left the luxury of palace service to rebuild Jerusalem's walls, stone by stone, amidst criticism and threats. *"What they are building—even a fox climbing up on it would break down their wall of stones!"* his enemies mocked (Nehemiah 4:3). Nehemiah didn't strike back. He prayed. He pressed on. He refused to let ridicule derail a divine assignment. He knew what God had placed in his heart, and no external voice could drown it out.

Paul wrote letters from prison cells. He endured beatings, betrayals, shipwrecks, and slander. Yet in 2 Timothy 4:7, he declared, *"I have fought the good fight, I have finished the race, I have kept the faith."* His vision was never about becoming known. It was about making Christ known.

Their fame wasn't of this world.

Today, vision still looks like quiet obedience. Like the mother who teaches Scripture to her children when no one is watching. Like the small-church pastor faithfully serving a dozen members with the same passion as if it were twelve thousand. Like the businessman who chooses truth over compromise.

The modern world rewards hype: the sudden, the dramatic, the attention-grabbing. Heaven rewards faithfulness. The spotlight isn't a measure of obedience. Some of the most impactful Kingdom builders will never trend, they're too busy building in secret what will one day last for generations.

The good news is Heaven sees what the world scrolls past.

Building for Applause

There's a season in my life when I had this completely backward.

Before I owned my company, I worked as a supervisor at a competing business. I took pride in my skill, my work ethic, and my leadership. I poured myself into becoming valuable, not just to the business, but to those around me. Recall the conversation I had with my former boss? Years later, when I stepped into ownership and began building something new, I needed a specific industry license that required a formal reference. Naturally, I reached out to my former boss. He knew my skill. He had seen my work. It should've been a simple yes.

He declined to help.

I assumed the worst: that it was because I was now in competition with him. It felt personal, and it planted something bitter in my heart. I still found a way to secure the license, but the rejection stung deeper than I admitted.

Months passed. Then, out of nowhere, he called me. He confessed his real reason for saying no. It wasn't about competition. It was fear, pride, and regret. He asked for forgiveness.

I didn't want to forgive him. Not then. Not yet. In my mind, he had tried to block my path, limit my family's future, and withhold something he knew I had earned. That pain turned into fuel. I made it my mission to outperform him in every possible way: business, leadership, family, friendships. I was going to become the man he only claimed to be. I climbed. I succeeded. I rose to the top of our industry.

I was burning out.

I couldn't sleep. I snapped at my kids. Wins felt hollow. Every day started with anxiety and ended with exhaustion. I wore the success like armor, but it didn't guard my soul. It only masked the cracks.

Then God spoke.

A whisper to my heart, but it landed with weight. "This is not yours. It's Mine. What belongs to Me cannot be stopped. Stop chasing shadows and focus on Me. I'll bless your effort, but only when My will comes first."

That day was another turning point. I had become arrogant. I had chased victory, not vision. It left me empty. So, I laid it down: the ambition, the bitterness, the performance trap. I said, "You're right! This business is Yours, not mine. Not his. Not anyone's but Yours. Do with it as you see. Use me through it as you see fit."

From that point on, everything shifted. My leadership changed. My peace returned and the vision grew clearer than ever.

When You Don't See the Results

Vision tests you. Not in the moment it's received, but in the months, years, and even decades that follow. Especially when the results don't match the revelation.

It's one thing to believe in God's promise when momentum is on your side. What about when the doors stay shut? When the numbers don't grow? When someone else receives the opportunities you prayed for? In those moments, the temptation to pivot, to try something flashier or faster, can feel overwhelming. Kingdom vision isn't tested by how fast it produces. It's tested by whether you'll stay faithful when it doesn't.

I love Joseph's story. It's truly the perfect case study. At seventeen, he saw a vision from God: wheat bowing, stars bending; greatness was being prophesied. What followed wasn't glory. It was a hell on Earth.

Slavery. Then false accusation followed by prison. For years, nothing about Joseph's life looked like his calling. He was a teenager with a divine vision, but for over a decade, he was invisible to the world. He was a slave, a servant, and a prisoner. In Genesis 39:2, the Scripture reminds us: *"The Lord was with Joseph so that he prospered... and the Lord gave him success in everything he did."*

This wasn't because he went viral or had a massive platform. It was because he stayed faithful in the shadows. The vision was real. The process was required. God wasn't slow; He was precise, using the season of obscurity to forge the character necessary to steward the blessing. It took nearly 30 years for Joesph's vision to grow to fruition.

Maybe you've poured your heart into a business or ministry, but no one seems to notice. Maybe you've obeyed God's leading, only to be met with resistance. Maybe you're wondering if you misheard Him because the outcome hasn't matched the obedience.

Let me say this: delayed results aren't denied calling.

"So is my word that goes out from my mouth: It will not return to me empty, but will accomplish what I desire and achieve the purpose for which I sent it." — Isaiah 55:11

If God said it, He will do it. Just know, He'll do it in His time, not yours.

Sometimes the delay is the very thing that forges the character you'll need for the next stage. Remember, David was anointed king long before he wore a crown. Jesus spent thirty years in obscurity before three years of ministry. Paul spent over a decade in preparation before planting churches. God isn't just preparing the platform; He is preparing the person.

Faithfulness isn't wasted in the Kingdom.

What Are You Really Building?

There's a haunting moment in Jesus' Sermon on the Mount where He says:

"Many will say to me on that day, 'Lord, Lord, did we not prophesy in your name… and in your name perform many miracles?' Then I will tell them plainly, 'I never knew you. Away from me, you evildoers!'" — Matthew 7:22–23

Let that settle in. These weren't rebels. These were people with platforms, with results. They had crowds, ministry success, at least from the outside. However, their work wasn't rooted in intimacy. Their "build" didn't begin with the Builder.

Jesus follows that warning with a parable: one man builds his house on the rock, another on sand. Both build; Both have a structure. Yet only one stands when the storm comes. Why? Foundation.

Vision without foundation is vanity. It's building a house on a fault line. It may look impressive, but it's destined to fall apart. Building on the rock means your purpose is rooted in a personal, intimate relationship with Christ. It means your worth isn't in your work, but in your identity as His child. The sand, on the other hand, is the shifting foundation of culture, trends, and the approval of the world.

I ask, what are you building? A brand? A legacy? A following? Are you building something for the world to admire, or something Heaven will recognize?

It's easy to slap God's name on our dreams and call it Kingdom. If you stripped away the platform, the income, the applause; would you still build? Would you still obey? Would you still steward what God has placed in your hands?

Real builders don't wait for an audience. They move when God speaks. They obey when it's inconvenient. They show up in silence, hammering away at something no one else can see.

They know that if God gave the vision, He'll sustain it whether or not it goes viral.

Faithfulness Is the New Fame

In the economy of Heaven, faithfulness is the highest currency. When God describes great servants in Scripture, He doesn't say, "Well done, good and popular servant." He says, *"Well done, good and faithful servant." — Matthew 25:21*

That's what He is looking for: not the flash, but the follow-through.

There's a quiet kind of greatness that never makes headlines. It's the business owner who operates with integrity, even when it costs a contract. It's the parent who disciples their children in the Word while the world says no. It's the leader who tells the truth, even when silence would sell better.

That's Kingdom fame.

Not being known by many but being known by God.

There's a verse tucked away in Zechariah 4:10 that says, *"Do not despise these small beginnings, for the Lord rejoices to see the work begin."* God rejoices not when something trends, but when something begins in obedience.

The world may never celebrate your obedience. Heaven throws a party for it.

The fruit of that kind of life lasts.

Jesus said in John 15:16, *"I chose you and appointed you so that you might go and bear fruit, fruit that will last."* That's what this is about. Not hype. Not hustle. Not metrics. Lasting fruit.

The Modern Builder

In the late 1960s, a pastor and seminary professor named Eugene Peterson began writing a new kind of Bible paraphrase. He worked on it quietly for decades, with no ambition for it to become a bestseller. His work was for his small congregation in Maryland who were struggling to connect with the ancient language of Scripture.

He didn't build it for virality. He built it for a vision: to help everyday people hear God's voice again. It was a slow, painstaking labor of love. When it finally gained traction, The Message Bible became one of the most widely read Bible translations in modern history, connecting with a generation that traditional versions had left behind. Peterson's story is a powerful reminder that building what lasts often happens far from the spotlight, in the quiet, consistent faithfulness of one person committed to a God-breathed vision.

Lasting Words

You weren't created to be popular. You were created to be planted.

Rooted.

Unshakable.

Fruit-bearing.

If no one sees?

Build it anyway.

WALK IT OUT

Protecting Your Vision

To protect your vision is to guard what God has revealed with both faith and discipline. Vision is fragile when it's new, and the wrong voices can cloud what heaven made clear. Begin by anchoring your vision in prayer. Bring it before God daily, not to seek constant change, but to stay aligned with His direction. Ask Him to refine your motives until His purpose is the only reason you pursue it. Vision grows strongest in stillness before it stands in visibility.

Create a record of what God has shown you. Write it out, speak it, and revisit it often. When the journey feels slow, your written words will remind you of what you're building and why it matters. Keep your notes private if needed, sharing only with those who carry faith equal to your own. The fewer the opinions, the clearer the focus.

Protect your heart from comparison. Every builder's timeline looks different, and your pace is not proof of your worth. Resist the temptation to measure progress by popularity or platform. Focus on the fruit that only faithfulness can produce. The unseen seasons are where God shapes your strength for what's ahead.

As you walk this process, let purity guide your strategy. Ask yourself regularly, "Does this decision protect what God planted, or does it expose it too soon?" Stay patient. A vision that's rushed can lose its foundation, while a vision that's refined through prayer and humility gains endurance. When you choose to protect your vision through obedience and restraint, God will expand it beyond what your effort could ever achieve.

CHAPTER SIX
Seed, Not Speed

The Slow Work of God Builds What Lasts.

"To everything there is a season, a time for every purpose under heaven." — Ecclesiastes 3:1

In the Kingdom of God, slow isn't a setback, it's a setup. This idea might sound absurd to a world that prizes acceleration. Our culture values speed like currency: faster delivery, quicker success, immediate answers. If it's not happening now, it must not be working. If it doesn't scale rapidly, it must not be worth building.

This obsession with speed has crept into our souls, subtly shaping how we evaluate our progress, our influence, and even our calling. The Kingdom doesn't operate on hustle time; it moves on harvest time. It doesn't sprint toward success; it sows. It doesn't panic under pressure; it plants with patience. In God's economy, there is purpose in the process, and the soil always matters more than the spotlight.

When Jesus described the Kingdom, He didn't compare it to lightning or wind or a wildfire. He compared it to a seed, a mustard seed, small and unimpressive, a farmer sowing into unseen soil. This sacred metaphor offers a quiet rebuke of our rush, the truth that real growth takes time, and rushing God's process only uproots what He is trying to establish.

The farmer plants the seed and then trusts the unseen process. He doesn't spend his days digging up the ground to check if the seed has sprouted. He knows that doing so would destroy the very life he is hoping to cultivate. This is a profound discipline, the ability to be patient, to trust God's timing, and to rest in the knowledge that He is working in the unseen. True spiritual maturity is found not in the speed of our output, but in the depth of our faith. It's in the waiting that our character is forged and our dependence on God is strengthened.

The Seduction of Speed

Speed promises success without sanctification. It lures you with efficiency but robs you of intimacy. The faster you go, the less likely you are to notice the hand of God moving slowly, steadily, and supernaturally in the background.

Many Kingdom entrepreneurs burn out not from a lack of vision but from an addiction to pace. Somewhere along the way, they start measuring fruitfulness by visibility, forgetting that Kingdom work often grows in hidden places long before it bears public fruit. What feels like a delay may be divine protection.

God rarely rushes those He calls. Moses waited forty years in the wilderness. Joseph endured betrayal and prison before promotion. Even Jesus spent thirty years in obscurity before His three years of ministry. If the Son of God Himself wasn't in a hurry, why are we? A rush to the top can expose our weaknesses and leave us without the character needed to sustain success. God's timing is always designed to forge us into the kind of leaders who can handle what He's entrusted to us.

Speed may get you attention but surrender births anointing. Acceleration isn't always advancement; sometimes it's avoidance. The fastest way to miss God's best is to move ahead of His timing. The allure of speed is often the voice of the enemy, urging us to rely on our own strength and strategies instead of leaning on God's divine provision. This path of self-reliance leads to spiritual and emotional exhaustion. The true power of the Kingdom is found not in our frantic efforts but in our peaceful trust.

You Can't Microwave a Miracle

The miracle God wants to do in your business, your purpose, your legacy is a slow-cooker kind of miracle. It's the kind that takes root before it bears fruit. No microwave can replicate the depth of what God develops in time.

We live in a world of instant coffee, instant fame, and instant downloads. There's no instant anointing; you can't microwave maturity. You can't get integrity with overnight shipping. You can't binge-watch your way into a legacy. The things that last take longer to form, and that's by divine design.

That's why God often gives you the seed instead of the tree. It's not a punishment; it's a process. When He gives you a seed, He's giving you a promise, but He's also inviting you into a partnership. He wants to see if you'll steward what's small, stay faithful when it's invisible, and still worship when it hasn't yet sprouted.

The seed isn't a shortcut; it's a start. The journey from seed to harvest is filled with unseen work. The roots must grow deep to support the future growth above ground. This unseen work is where the true character of a leader is forged. The microwave mentality of instant gratification only creates shallow, temporary results.

God's process is a divine partnership. He provides the seed, the vision, the calling, the promise, and you provide the faithfulness, the patience, and the diligence to sow it. He does the growing, but you must do the waiting. The miracle is not just in the harvest; it's in the transformation that happens within you during the process.

The Faith of a Farmer

One of Jesus' most quietly powerful parables is found in Mark 4. The parable of the Sower.

"This is what the kingdom of God is like. A man scatters seed on the ground. Night and day, whether he sleeps or gets up, the seed sprouts and grows, though he does not know how." — Mark 4:26-27

That line, *"though he does not know how,"* is one of the most encouraging and humbling verses in all of Scripture. It reminds us that growth is God's responsibility. Your job is to sow. His job is to grow.

My close friend, Tom, worked for an HR firm that, seemingly overnight, went out of business. Tom was soon answering panicked calls from his personal clients. They were nervous, and he was nervous. He was just a salesman. He hadn't run this type of business before, so what could he do to help?

Tom went to prayer with God, the one who gives the increase. He then reached out individually to each client and made a promise, "Stay with me and I'll handle it." He decided he would learn everything about HR and payroll. He would no longer be the salesman; he would be the leader his clients needed. Not all the clients stayed on board. Some abandoned ship. However, those who stayed did so because of the trust they had in Tom, trust that was built over time. It took some time to iron out all the details, but Tom accomplished his goal for his clients and himself. The journey wasn't quick, but it did result in good fruit. Tom's agency is now thriving and he's doing very well.

Remember, God is not impressed by how fast you can build; He's pleased by how well you can trust. That's why He sometimes delays what you desire, so you can develop the faith to carry what you'll one day receive. He's not just building your business, He's building you. This is the essence of true Kingdom work, not a frantic scramble for success, but a peaceful partnership with God.

The farmer's faith is a powerful example for us, teaching us to release our need for control and to embrace a posture of trust. This trust is cultivated in the quiet moments of waiting. It's in the seasons of silence, when nothing seems to be happening, that our faith is most profoundly tested and strengthened.

The Death in the Dirt

Every seed goes through a burial before it ever sees breakthrough. It's in the burial where the magic happens, where it dies to its shell.

"Very truly I tell you, unless a kernel of wheat falls to the ground and dies, it remains only a single seed. But if it dies, it produces many seeds." —John 12:24

You'll have seasons where you feel buried, forgotten, hidden, and still. You're not buried to be punished; you're planted to be prepared. The slow seasons aren't void of value. They're where identity is refined, motives are tested, and character is deepened.

You don't skip the soil; you grow through it. The burial is a necessary part of the process. It's in the dark, silent soil that the seed's potential is unleashed. It's in the seasons of obscurity that God prunes away what is not essential, preparing you for the growth to come. The death of the seed is not a finality; it's a promise of new life, a new beginning, a new harvest.

Your Seed Carries Future Generations

When you sow Kingdom seed, you're not just investing in your business or your impact. You're planting something that can outlive you. The seed may not grow fast, but it will grow deep; and the deeper it goes, the more it can sustain.

The decisions you make today, the values you protect, the excellence you model, the obedience you walk in, those are seeds. They may not seem like much now, but ten years from now, they could become the standard by which others lead. Fifty years from now, they might be the fruit that nourishes generations.

God is looking for leaders who aren't addicted to applause but are anchored in purpose. Leaders who would rather be faithful in the field than famous on social media. Leaders who sow with a legacy in mind. The seed doesn't just serve you; it carries a harvest that your children's children may one day reap. This is the ultimate goal of Kingdom work: to build a legacy that transcends our own lifespan. When we shift our focus from immediate gratification to generational impact, our priorities change. We're no longer driven by the desire for quick wins, but by the commitment to building something that will last.

From Panic to Provision

I remember a moment early in our business journey when my wife asked me with genuine concern in her voice, "How are we going to make what we need every day?" At the time, our goal was just $1,200 a day. That number felt enormous to her, and honestly, at that point, it truly was. She wasn't sure how that kind of income could consistently come in. While I wasn't worried about our ability to do the work and earn the money, I was nervous about something else entirely: Would people even want what we offered, every single day, all year long?

We both had different fears, but we learned the same lesson quickly: when we stay faithful to God, He takes care of the rest. Today, we need several times that amount every day just to operate, and not only does it happen, but it doesn't feel impossible for it to grow even more. That's what happens when you plant in obedience and trust the seed. The shift in perspective from panic to provision didn't happen in a single moment; it was a gradual process of learning to trust God's faithfulness over our own frantic efforts.

The Kingdom Isn't a Startup

God's plan for your life is not a startup business; it's a generational mission. He's not looking for overnight disruption. He's looking for long-haul faithfulness. The Kingdom doesn't operate like Silicon Valley. There are no IPOs for obedience. There are no "exit strategies" for purpose.

In startup culture, success is often measured by speed, how fast you can build, scale, flip, and sell. In the Kingdom, success is measured by fruit: how deeply you've rooted, how faithfully you've stewarded, and how fully you've obeyed. God is not calling you to launch and exit; He's calling you to plant and remain. If you want Kingdom outcomes, you must reject worldly metrics. You're not building for investors; you're building for eternity.

When you embrace the slowness of God's timing, you begin to live in rhythm with Heaven. You stop obsessing over quarterly growth and start focusing on generational impact. You stop chasing hype and start cultivating holiness. That shift changes everything. The Kingdom model is not about making a quick buck; it's about making a lasting impact. It's not about being the first to market; it's about being faithful in the field.

Don't Rush What God Is Writing

You were not created for quick wins; you were created for eternal fruit. Kingdom work often looks slow in the beginning, but that's because God is writing a story that lasts longer than a single season.

Don't measure your progress by the pace of others. The world may sprint, but the Spirit sows. The soil God places you in isn't a punishment; it's preparation. When you feel unseen, keep sowing. When you feel uncelebrated, stay faithful. When you feel like nothing is happening, remember, the most important things often start in the unseen.

The slow seasons are where God is doing His most important work, not in your business, but in you.

WALK IT OUT

Learning To Wait Well

To learn to wait well is to trust that delay can be divine. Waiting in the Kingdom is not wasted time; it's sacred preparation. Every seed has a season, and God's process can't be rushed without losing depth. Begin by shifting how you see waiting. It's not a pause in progress but a classroom where faith matures. Ask God to teach you what He's building in you while you wait for what He's building around you.

During these seasons, stay engaged with the work already before you. Do what's in your hand while trusting Him with what's in your heart. Patience grows stronger when it's paired with action. When you remain faithful to the task you have now, you demonstrate that you're ready for the responsibility He's preparing next.

Thank God daily for lessons learned, for hidden development, and for unseen growth. Gratitude turns waiting from frustration into worship. It shifts your attention from what's missing to what's forming. Those who wait well always emerge with stronger roots and steadier faith.

Protect your heart from comparison. Others may appear to be moving faster, but speed has never been a sign of favor. Stay rooted where God planted you. Water your field with prayer, diligence, and gratitude until He says it's time to harvest. When the appointed season arrives, you'll realize the wait was never punishment; it was preparation for a blessing that required maturity to sustain. Waiting well trains you to trust His timing more than your own and to believe that what grows slowly often lasts the longest.

CHAPTER SEVEN
Obedience Over Opportunity

Not Every Open Door Is a God-Door.

"Very truly I tell you, the Son can do nothing by himself; he can do only what he sees his Father doing." —John 5:19

Our culture screams, "Chase every opportunity!" However, not every open door is divine. Many are distractions dressed in urgency. The pressure to act, respond, launch, and scale can look like wisdom, but if God didn't send you, it's just noise disguised as strategy. Jesus modeled a counter-cultural principle: He didn't act on demand. He acted on direction. His movements were slow, Spirit-led, and often misunderstood by the crowds who wanted more from Him.

If opportunity were the highest measure of success, Jesus would have had the busiest calendar in history. Crowds pressed in. Towns begged Him to stay. There was always another person to heal, another message to preach, another urgent need demanding His presence. However, Jesus lived by a deeper rhythm, one that confounds our obsession with hustle and performance. He only did what the Father told Him to do.

He didn't say yes to every request. He didn't measure impact by popularity. He walked past needs because His life was governed not by open doors, but by divine direction. In a world that trains us to chase visibility, the discipline of obedience is radical. It means you'll have to say no to opportunities that flatter your ego. You'll walk away from positions that seem perfect on paper. You'll risk being misunderstood, overlooked, or even criticized, not because you're lazy, but because you're loyal. This loyalty is to a higher purpose, a divine mission often invisible to the world. It's a quiet conviction that what God has for you is better than what the world offers.

Where in your life is the pressure of an open door competing with the pull of divine direction?

The Counterintuitive Call

Obedience will often look like failure to everyone else. It won't always feel strategic. It won't always make financial sense. Heaven doesn't promote the clever; it promotes the faithful. The world sees a closed door as a loss, but in the Kingdom, it can be a divine redirection, a quiet protection from a path that would have taken you off course.

A Kingdom leader must resist the gravitational pull of doing more simply because they can. Just because you have the skills or resources to take on another project doesn't mean you're called to it. The real question isn't, "Is this a good opportunity?" but "Has God assigned this to me?"

You'll have to say no to opportunities that flatter your ego. This isn't about false humility; it's about discerning whether the applause feeds your identity or aligns with Heaven's agenda.

We confuse giftedness with calling all the time. Gifts are tools. Assignments are mandates. If you operate in someone else's assignment, even if you do it well, you may forfeit what's meant for your own. Your gifts are meant to serve your assignment, not define it. A surgeon is gifted, but if he tries to use his gift on a construction site, he is misaligned and ineffective. The same is true in the Kingdom. Your God-given strength is tied to your assignment.

Are you operating in your calling, or just using your gifts?

Obedience Isn't Always Efficient

It would have been more efficient for Jesus to stay in one city, build a mega-ministry, and attract thousands. He kept moving, sometimes at what looked like the worst possible time. At other moments, He waited when momentum was building. His actions often went against what a Silicon Valley consultant might advise.

The obedience walk isn't streamlined. It's sacred. It doesn't bow to the pressure of performance. It walks at the pace of the Spirit. However, that pace feels too slow for our liking.

We like to move when there's energy. God often speaks in the stillness. We want clarity. God says, "Follow Me."

The world operates on a timeline of deliverables and deadlines. The Kingdom operates on a timeline of seasons and faithfulness. The most profound work God does is often a slow, deliberate process that defies our human need for efficiency. This is why the discipline of waiting is vital. Waiting on God is not passive; it's an active, prayerful posture of trust. It's the moment where you say, "I could move forward on my own, but I will wait for Your clear direction."

What is the quietest thing God has ever asked you to do?

Obedience Requires Inner Stillness

One of the greatest obstacles to obedience isn't rebellion; it's noise. When the internal clamor of fear, ambition, and comparison drowns out divine whispers, obedience becomes almost impossible. To hear God's voice, you must first quiet your own.

Obedience begins with alignment. You must train your spirit to listen and then be okay with silence. You must sit with uncertainty and discern God's nudge, even when the data says otherwise. This is the radical discipline of a Kingdom leader. This inner stillness is not a luxury; it's a necessity. It's the soil in which conviction grows.

This is how Kingdom people lead. Not with charts and checklists, but with conviction. Not with trends, but with truth. Not with charisma, but with character. You're not a CEO in Heaven's eyes. You're a steward. This isn't a demotion; it's a reorientation. CEOs cast vision; stewards execute the owner's will. That distinction will reshape every decision, from your daily tasks to your greatest risks. A steward knows that what they have isn't their own. They're not building their own empire but faithfully managing the resources and assignments of another. This reorientation takes the pressure off performance and places the focus on faithfulness.

The Discipline of Saying No

We've been taught to believe that saying no is selfish, ungrateful, or lazy. However, a well-placed no is often the most obedient act of your life. It's an act of spiritual warfare, a statement that you will not be led astray by the seductive lure of opportunity.

It guards your mission, protects your margin, and honors your calling.

Some of the greatest breakthroughs in your life will come from what you refused to do, not what you've added on. The power of "no" is the power to stay focused, to protect your God-given strength, and to remain in the lane God has assigned to you.

When Nehemiah was building the wall, distractions came dressed as invitations. He had political rivals, Sanballat and Tobiah, who wanted to draw him away from his great work. They sent messages to him saying, *"Come, let us meet together in one of the villages on the plain of Ono."*

Nehemiah knew their intentions were malicious and their "invitation" was a distraction from his assignment. He sent back a simple reply: *"I am doing a great work and I cannot come down. Why should the work stop while I leave it and come down to you?"* — Nehemiah 6:2-3

That's the discernment of obedience, the ability to recognize that distraction doesn't always come as sin. Sometimes it comes as options. Saying yes to one thing means saying no to another. The yes may cost you more than the no.

The High Cost of Disobedience

It's tempting to think delayed obedience is harmless. Waiting a little longer or tweaking the plan can seem minor. However, delayed obedience is still disobedience. Even in small doses, it has a ripple effect.

Ask Jonah. His detour didn't just affect him; it endangered others. When you say yes to what God didn't assign, someone else, a client, a teammate, a family is left waiting, their answer delayed. Your disobedience can create chaos and confusion in the lives of those around you.

Obedience is never about you alone. It's generational. It's interwoven with destinies you can't even see yet. Every obedient step you take today is a seed sown for a future harvest that will bless generations to come. Every disobedient step, however small, can become a stumbling block for those who are meant to follow you.

Who is waiting on you to be obedient?

When I Chose the Wrong Yes

There was a season where my obedience had a competitor. When my wife and I bought our company, I had all the right language. I said it was about building something God could use. I prayed over decisions. I asked for wisdom. Beneath it all, however, I had a second motive I didn't want to admit: I wanted to prove myself.

Years earlier, I had worked under a supervisor who made it clear that I was replaceable. When I left, I carried that wound into my new role. I wanted to outperform him. Outgrow him. Outshine him. For a while, it looked like I did. The business exploded. Our reputation grew. We reached milestones that should have made me proud.

I wasn't at peace. I wasn't fulfilled. I wasn't truly free. I had said yes to an opportunity, but no to obedience. I had followed ambition instead of instruction. My own ego had become the compass, and the destination was a hollow kind of success. God, in His mercy, let it unravel just enough to get my attention. It was a painful but necessary process. The weight of my self-made success became unbearable. When it did, I realized something sobering: this wasn't my business to prove anything with. It was His. The burden I'd unknowingly carried for years suddenly lifted, replaced by a profound sense of peace and purpose.

That shift changed everything. I stopped building to prove and started building to please. I let go of the scoreboard and picked up the assignment again. The experience taught me that the biggest opportunities are often the ones that lead us back to the heart of God, not away from it.

Obedience Bears Eternal Fruit

Hustle gives quick results. Obedience produces enduring fruit. The world celebrates the quick harvest, but the Kingdom celebrates the deep roots. The business deal you walked away from because it lacked integrity preserved your character, which will bear fruit in every future partnership. The contract you didn't sign because it came with compromise safeguarded your long-term influence and peace. The stage you declined because your character wasn't ready cultivated the authority needed for a future, more impactful platform.

These are the moments that seem small in the eyes of the world but echo in eternity. The world's metrics are fleeting, but God's metrics are eternal. He's not just looking at the scoreboard; He is looking at the soil of your soul. God doesn't reward productivity; He rewards faithfulness. We will give an account not for how many things we built, but for whether we built what He told us to. This redefines success from what we achieve to who we become in the process.

What fruit are you trying to force that God wants to cultivate?

Trusting God When Obedience Doesn't Pay Yet

There's a tension most faith-driven leaders eventually face, obeying God when it looks like it's not working. You follow His voice and say no to a major client, and your bank account gets tighter. You choose integrity over shortcuts, and someone else gets the promotion. You stay committed to a small vision, while everyone else seems to be scaling and winning.

This is the ache of obedience. When what God asks you to do doesn't immediately reward you, it's easy to doubt. Faith, however, isn't measured by results; it's measured by trust. Obedience is a prophetic declaration: *I trust You more than I trust my own plans.*

Sometimes, Heaven delays the results to deepen the roots. If you only obey for the outcome, then it's not obedience; it's a transaction. God isn't interested in a transactional relationship; He is interested in an intimate one. He wants to know that you will follow Him for who He is, not just for what He can give you.

How Obedience Shapes Leadership

Leadership in the Kingdom doesn't begin with charisma, strategy, or a compelling vision; it begins at the feet of Jesus. It begins in the quiet, hidden place of surrender. Before you can lead anyone else with clarity, you must be led by the King with conviction. Obedience is not just a spiritual checkbox; it's a furnace that forges character, softens pride, and sharpens discernment. It teaches your spirit to stay humble, available, and aligned with Heaven's agenda, not your own.

People can feel the difference. Your team can sense when your confidence comes from submission, not ambition. Your clients recognize when your "yes" isn't just a pitch; it carries the weight of conviction. Your decisions begin to carry a wisdom that can't be explained by spreadsheets alone. Your presence begins to shift atmospheres, not because you're impressive, but because you're entrusted.

Kingdom leadership isn't something you hustle for; it's something you're entrusted with. It comes not from being the loudest in the room but from being the most surrendered. It's a quiet, immovable confidence, the kind that only comes from walking in step with the Spirit.

People don't just follow what you say. They follow the weight behind it. That weight only comes when Heaven is backing your steps.

What You Refuse to Do Defines You

Our culture is obsessed with what people do: the businesses they start, the influence they gain, the accolades they collect. In the Kingdom, however, what you refuse to do is just as important. Jesus refused to make a name for Himself. He refused to let the crowd define His mission. He refused to let Peter talk Him out of the cross. What you turn down becomes a testimony. It tells the world, "I'm not for sale." That's power.

There's strength in your restraint. Holiness in your hesitation. Authority in your boundaries. The next time you're tempted to justify a compromise, remember: your "no" might be your greatest ministry. It's a sign that you're a person of integrity, and that integrity is a powerful witness to a world that has lost its way.

When Obedience Feels Lonely

One of the hardest parts of obedience is how isolating it can feel. Everyone else is going left, and you're being asked to go right. Everyone else is moving fast, and God has you waiting. Everyone else is building wide, and you're still digging deep.

That tension isn't punishment. It's preparation. You're being shaped in the quiet. Tested in obscurity. Rooted in silence. Not for your own sake, but for the sake of what, and who, you're called to carry. Obedience will always cost you something. Disobedience will cost you far more. The loneliness of obedience is a sign that you're on the right path, a path that is narrow and less traveled. It's a path that leads to life.

Consider the example of C.S. Lewis. A brilliant, respected academic, he could have spent his entire career in the comfortable, prestigious world of Oxford. God, however, called him to write Christian apologetics, a pursuit often looked down upon by his intellectual peers. His obedience led to a quiet, steady output of work that would eventually reach millions. He said no to the opportunity of purely academic fame in favor of an assignment from God, and that singular act of obedience still bears fruit today. His legacy isn't in his professorship, but in his faithfulness.

Lasting Words

There are God-given strengths you'll never unlock until you walk through the door obedience opens.

On the other side of your yes is provision. On the other side is peace. On the other side is the supernatural, not just for your business, but for your soul.

You don't need to see the full map. You don't need to understand every step. You just need to walk the one path God has placed in front of you.

Say yes. Even if it's slow; even if it's quiet. Even if it costs you everything.

If obedience costs you the world but gives you Jesus, it's never a loss.

WALK IT OUT

Choosing The Narrow Door

To choose the narrow door is to live with discernment when opportunity calls. Not every open door leads to destiny, and not every invitation carries God's endorsement. Culture celebrates volume—the more projects, the better, but the Kingdom celebrates precision. Begin by asking God for the wisdom to recognize His voice in every decision. Before you say yes, pause to listen. Pray, "Lord, is this door Yours for me, or is it simply open?" Peace will always confirm His path, while pressure often reveals distraction.

Choosing the narrow door requires humility, because it often looks smaller than the one you wanted. It may offer less attention or fewer rewards, yet it will always hold more anointing. Trust that God hides His best assignments in places that require faith to enter. When you follow peace rather than popularity, you trade quick progress for eternal fruit.

Learn to identify opportunities that pull you away from your purpose. If it drains your focus, divides your time, or distorts your values, it's not for you. Stay true to what God has already placed in your hands until He clearly gives you more. Saying no to the wrong door is often the first step toward the right one.

Keep your heart anchored in obedience. Ask the Holy Spirit to align your desires with God's will so that what tempts others doesn't distract you. When you learn to walk through narrow doors, you prove that you value God's direction more than man's approval. Over time, your confidence in His leading will silence the noise of every competing opportunity. The narrow path may feel costly, however it's where purpose deepens, peace lives, and the fruit of your labor lasts.

CHAPTER EIGHT
Marketplace Ministry

The False Divide.

"Whatever you do, work at it with all your heart, as working for the Lord, not for human masters." — Colossians 3:23

We've lived for too long with this artificial separation, a mental firewall dividing our lives into sacred and secular boxes. Sunday is for church, Monday is for the office. You pray in the morning, and you worry about payroll in the afternoon. Worship is for the sanctuary, but work is something else entirely. God, however, never intended for this duality to exist. He designed our work as a primary place for His presence and purpose to be revealed.

In the Kingdom, there is no real separation between ministry and the marketplace. Your calling isn't limited to a pulpit, and your assignment isn't restricted to a church building. In fact, some of the most profound Kingdom impact is meant to happen in boardrooms, on construction sites, in coffee shops, and from home offices.

At some point, we somehow adopted this false idea that spiritual work is more valuable than "regular" work. We started thinking pastors are the ones doing the real ministry, while business owners, salespeople, creators, and entrepreneurs are doing something second-rate. This is simply not true. It's a complete lie.

Remember; when God placed Adam in the Garden, His very first instruction wasn't to go plant a church; it was to get to work and cultivate.

"The Lord God took the man and put him in the Garden of Eden to work it and take care of it." — Genesis 2:15.

Work was never a curse; it was meant to be an act of worship, a form of co-creation and stewardship where humanity partnered with God. The fall of man certainly distorted work, making it toilsome and difficult, but it never, ever took away its sacred purpose.

This historical and theological context is critical. The Protestant Reformation, particularly through the teachings of Martin Luther and John Calvin, was one of the first major challenges to this sacred-secular divide. They championed the idea of a "calling," or vocation, that applied to every profession. A shoemaker could glorify God just as much as a priest. Their daily labor, performed with integrity and excellence, was seen as a form of worship. This powerful truth re-centered the Gospel in the everyday lives of believers, shifting the focus from a monastery to the marketplace. Your daily work, no matter how mundane or small it seems, is a stage for God's redemptive work.

Your Business Is Your Altar

You may never stand on a stage to preach, but you preach every single day just by how you run your business. Integrity is a message. Excellence is a powerful witness. The way you treat your employees, your clients, and your vendors speaks volumes about who you truly serve.

Do you ever cut corners when no one's watching?

Do you overpromise just to win contracts?

Do you strive for excellence even when it's not strictly required?

The way you handle these moments reveals whether your business is just a money-making machine or a true altar to the Lord.

Your business becomes your altar when you present your work

as a sacrifice of worship. For a creative director, this might mean honoring the budget and delivering on a promise even when the client is difficult. For a contractor, it means showing up on time, communicating delays transparently, and never cutting corners on materials. For a retail store owner, it means treating every customer with dignity, regardless of how big or small their purchase is.

An altar is a place of surrender and sacrifice, and when your business decisions are made with the same reverence you would show in a sanctuary, you're literally building an altar. This is the difference between a transactional business and a transformational one. The first is about what you get; the second is about what you give.

The Holy Spirit Belongs in the Office

The same Spirit that inspires a worship leader's song can strategically guide a CEO's vision. The same anointing that helps a preacher prepare a sermon can help a contractor solve a difficult problem, a designer dream up a new campaign, or a sales rep serve a client with genuine compassion. In *Exodus 31*, God filled Bezalel with the Spirit, not to preach, but to craft. The Spirit gave him the skill, ability, and creativity needed to build the tabernacle. That same Spirit is eager to equip you for spreadsheets, sales calls, and product launches.

We have for so long limited the Holy Spirit to "church work." He is wildly creative. He is strategic and wise, and He desperately wants to be invited into your daily operations. He wants to give you ideas no business school could ever teach. He wants to guide you through difficult team dynamics. He wants to birth solutions that literally reveal Heaven on earth.

Imagine a marketing campaign concept that comes to you in a quiet moment of prayer. A new business model is downloaded to you during a walk. A breakthrough solution to a manufacturing problem emerges from a time of worship. The Holy Spirit isn't just for our spiritual lives; He is the source of all wisdom and creativity, and He longs to be a true partner in your professional life.

You're a Pastor in Disguise

If you own a business or lead a team, you're shepherding people, whether you realize it or not. Your employees are watching you. Your customers are listening. Your vendors are paying attention. Your integrity, or lack of it, is preaching a sermon every single day. You may be the only Bible some people ever read. So, what are they learning about God from your leadership?

To shepherd means to guide, to protect, and to nurture. This applies directly to leadership in the marketplace. You guide your team toward a common vision. You protect them from burnout and unfair practices. You nurture their gifts and help them grow, both professionally and personally. Shepherding your team looks like creating a safe environment where they feel valued. It looks like celebrating their wins, not just in business but in their personal lives. It looks like praying for them by name, caring about their families, and helping them navigate seasons of hardship.

You don't have to use spiritual language for this to be a spiritual act. When you care for your people the way Christ cares for you, you're living out your calling as a pastor in disguise. Your greatest sermon may be the example you set, not the words you speak.

A Case for Holy Ambition

Sometimes faith-driven entrepreneurs shy away from ambition, afraid it's prideful or worldly. God-given ambition is neither. Holy ambition isn't about self-promotion; it's about God-exaltation through our stewardship and service. Ambition becomes Kingdom when it's fully submitted. When your drive is fueled by obedience, not ego. When growth is a vehicle for impact, not status. God isn't concerned with the size of your scale; He has an issue with idolatry. If you can steward success without it owning you, He can entrust you with even more.

Holy ambition is simply the desire to use your gifts and resources to their fullest potential for the glory of God and the good of others. It's the drive that propelled Queen Esther to risk her life to save her people, knowing she was *"created for such a time as this."*

It's the same drive that led William Wilberforce to spend decades fighting for the abolition of the slave trade. The danger isn't in the size of your ambition, but in the object of its worship. When your ambition is an act of worship, it becomes a powerful force for Kingdom good.

George Washington Carver, a scientist born into slavery who, after his freedom, turned down a prestigious corporate job to serve at a small, struggling institute in Alabama. His holy ambition wasn't for personal wealth or fame, but to use his gifts to help poor farmers escape poverty. His work with peanuts, sweet potatoes, and other crops transformed the agricultural landscape of the South and lifted countless families out of destitution. His life is a powerful testament to the idea that true success isn't found in what you accumulate, but in how you serve.

Excellence As Evangelism

Let's be honest; we've all heard the phrase "Christian business," and sometimes that term is loosely fitting. It's not enough to slap a Bible verse on your mission statement or play worship music in the lobby. Kingdom business isn't about branding; it's about behavior. Excellence is one of the most underused tools of evangelism. As Peter says, *"You are a chosen people, a royal priesthood, a holy nation, God's special possession, that you may declare the praises of him who called you out of darkness into his wonderful light."* — 1 Peter 2:9

When you show up prepared, deliver with integrity, treat people with honor, and follow through consistently, people will absolutely take notice. It won't be because you're loud about your faith, but because your fruit speaks for itself. Daniel didn't have to shout his beliefs. His excellence made him indispensable in a pagan kingdom.

What if we treated every customer as though we were serving Christ Himself? What if our contracts were our covenants? What if we prayed as hard about hiring decisions as we do about church decisions? That's the standard of the Kingdom. It should mark every spreadsheet, every service call, every creative draft.

Excellence isn't just about the final product; it's about the entire process. It's in the details. It's in the way you respond to a complaint, the way you own up to a mistake, and the way you go above and beyond what is required. When a client sees that you operate with a higher standard than the competition, not just in price but in quality and integrity, they'll eventually ask why.

That "why" is your open door to share the source of your values. Your work becomes a living testament to the God you serve.

Of course, I can't emphasize this enough: small details matter more than large ones. It's the small things that will build you up or tear you down. The big details, actions, or inactions are a result of accumulated small details directed one way or the other.

Business As a Discipleship Tool

The Great Commission isn't just for the pulpit. Jesus said, *"Go and make disciples of all nations..."* — *Matthew 28:19.* That includes corporate cultures, service sectors, and global industries.

When you create a business, you create a culture. You're shaping mindsets, habits, ethics, and values, sometimes more powerfully than a sermon ever could. Do your employees feel seen? Cared for? Challenged to grow? Do your clients encounter more than just professionalism; do they experience peace? Do your competitors see humility instead of cutthroat competition?

We all know the problem: the world of business is often defined by burnout, anxiety, and the constant pressure to perform. At our company, we saw the cost of this culture firsthand and decided to do something different. Our company operates on the principle of project completion over clocking hours. We schedule eight-hour workdays, but if our team finishes early, they reclaim that time.

In 2024 alone, our team collectively reclaimed over 360 hours, the equivalent of nine full work weeks. We could have assigned more tasks and used that time to generate more revenue, but we chose not to. Why? Because we believe reclaimed time is more valuable than additional income. We chose to let our team steward those hours however they needed; with their families, in rest, or in purpose. As a result, our company has flourished. Our people are thriving.

We're not just building a business; we're forming a culture. That culture is discipling hearts toward something better than burnout. Rest isn't a weakness. It's discipleship in motion. This is the kind of transformative culture that God wants to see in the marketplace. He wants you to build a place where people can encounter the values of the Kingdom in a tangible way.

Wealth With a Mission

Let's talk money, because it absolutely matters. There's nothing unholy about profit. In fact, God delights in blessing His children. Remember though, blessing without purpose becomes bondage.

Money is a tool, not a trophy. When it's placed in the hands of someone with Kingdom vision, it can change lives. The world teaches us to earn more for comfort. The Kingdom invites us to earn more for impact. What if your business wasn't just a source of income, but a source of generosity? What if profit allowed you to employ single moms, support missionaries, fund justice initiatives, or invest in community transformation? Wealth in the Kingdom is never just about accumulation; it's about activation. When you tie your financial goals to eternal outcomes, Heaven backs your hustle.

One example of this is David Green, the founder of Hobby Lobby. He started the business in his garage with just a $600 loan, and over time it became one of the largest arts and crafts retailers in the world. His vision was never just about retail; it was about impact. Green tithes generously, funds Bibles in multiple languages, supports Christian universities, and closes all stores on Sundays to honor the Sabbath. He once said, "This isn't our business; it's God's." When the government challenged his convictions on religious freedom, he didn't compromise. He stood firm and won.

David Green proves that it's possible to build big and still bow at His feet. When Kingdom values are woven into every level of leadership, business becomes one of the most powerful tools for ministry. David didn't see his company as an end, but as a vehicle for God's purposes.

When Faith Costs You in the Marketplace

Let's not pretend obedience is always easy. Living out your faith in business can cost you a deal, a relationship, or a platform. Sometimes, your refusal to bend on ethical lines will label you as difficult or inflexible. Other times, the decisions you make out of conviction will confuse or even alienate others. Here's what you must always remember: God sees. He sees when you refund a client even though you didn't have to. He sees when you walk away from a shady vendor deal or when you honor the Sabbath, even when it hurts your metrics.

You will never lose with God what you lay down in obedience.

There's a joy that comes from honoring God in your business, even when it costs you something. Over time, your reputation becomes a magnet. People will seek you out not just because of your product or pricing, but because they trust your name. Your integrity becomes a form of marketing more powerful than any ad campaign you could ever run.

Lasting Words

You're not just a business owner; you're not just an employee. You're an ambassador of the Kingdom, placed by God in a sphere that desperately needs the light you carry. Don't just manage, shepherd. Don't just scale; steward. Don't just close deals; create culture.

You may never hold a microphone, but your work ethic is your message, your generosity is your Gospel, and your integrity is a sermon in shoes.

Go, make the hire, take the risk, and launch the vision. Just make sure Jesus is at the center of it all.

If your business becomes your platform but not your altar, you've completely missed the point. If your work becomes your worship, your business becomes a vessel for Heaven to move.

The Spirit of God doesn't require a stage to move; He just needs a surrendered vessel. This means your office can be an altar, your job site can be a mission field, and your Zoom meeting can become sacred ground. Why? Because your work isn't just work; it's worship.

Don't downplay your calling just because it doesn't look like someone else's. Your obedience is shaking eternity in ways you may never fully see on this side of Heaven.

This isn't just business; it's Kingdom business.

CHAPTER EIGHT

That changes everything.

WALK IT OUT

Carrying The Kingdom to Work

To carry the Kingdom to work is to see your profession as your platform for ministry. The Kingdom is not confined to the church; it flows wherever God's people are sent. Begin by recognizing that your job, trade, or business is a mission field. You represent Christ long before you ever mention His name. Every conversation, decision, and attitude becomes an opportunity to reflect His nature.

Start each day by inviting the Holy Spirit to walk with you through your workday. Ask Him for wisdom before meetings, patience in conflict, and creativity in problem-solving. When you depend on His presence, your workplace becomes an altar where excellence and grace coexist. Excellence earns trust, and trust opens hearts. Through consistent integrity, others begin to see the difference God makes in the way you lead, serve, and respond.

Refuse to separate your faith from your function. Let the way you work become your testimony. Be the one who arrives early, honors your word, and treats every person with respect. Pray quietly for the people around you, even the difficult ones. Ask God to use your life as evidence of His peace in chaotic environments.

As you carry the Kingdom into your work, focus on impact rather than image. The goal isn't to be known for your faith; it's to make Him known through your faithfulness. When you view work as worship, ordinary tasks take on eternal significance. You're no longer just clocking hours or closing deals. You're cultivating influence that reveals the goodness of God wherever He's placed you. Carrying the Kingdom to work transforms your career from a paycheck into a calling, and your workplace into a field ready for harvest.

CHAPTER NINE
Provision Follows Purpose

He Funds What He Assigns.

"But seek first his kingdom and his righteousness, and all these things will be given to you as well." — Matthew 6:33

What if your greatest fear is also your greatest invitation? The fear of lack is a quiet struggle for many faith-driven builders. It's the voice that whispers just as you take a step: Will there be enough? Enough to make payroll, enough to bridge a slow season, enough to keep the household steady if the vision doesn't unfold as hoped? I know this fact personally. We've been there and done that.

The good news is that wherever God gives purpose, He also supplies provision. He is faithful to fund what He assigns, and He does so according to the wisdom of His timing. Provision never goes before purpose. It always follows.

The King's economy appears throughout Scripture as action before direction. Abraham didn't demand a fully labeled route before he packed his tent. He moved because God said go, and supply met him along the road. Moses didn't gather donors or draft a travel budget before facing Pharaoh. He entered the palace with a staff in his hand and a word in his mouth, and God matched his obedience with signs and favor that made an impossible release inevitable.

The first disciples didn't establish a fund to underwrite a three-year tour with Jesus. They left their nets, stepped into their assignment, and discovered that homes, meals, and help awaited them on the path of obedience.

The logic is simple. God's not a venture capitalist searching for the lowest risk and highest return. He's the King who provides for the assignments He gives. If the vision genuinely came from Him, the provision will ultimately flow from Him. That truth never excuses laziness or poor planning. It places planning in its proper order. Your first job isn't to fund the assignment; your first job is to obey it. Provision isn't the driver of the mission; provision becomes the passenger that climbs in once obedience puts the car in motion.

This order changes how we start things. We pray, we listen, and we test the assignment with Scripture and wise counsel. Then we move, not recklessly, but resolutely. We build budgets and timelines, yet we refuse to be paralyzed by the absence of total visibility. The King is responsible for the King's business. We're responsible for faithful steps.

The Illusion of Self-Made Success

Culture praises the self-made story. Work longer, grind harder, prove your worth. That script can motivate for a season, but it can't sustain a soul. In God's Kingdom, self-reliance isn't a badge of honor. It's a weight that eventually bends the back of the proud. Heaven isn't impressed when we demonstrate how much we can build without God. Heaven looks for the humble, the leaders who recognize their need for Him at every turn, who run decisions past His wisdom, and who treat success as stewardship rather than proof of superiority.

Success built on self becomes a fragile structure. It may deliver a larger house, a fuller calendar, or a louder platform, but it rarely delivers rest. When peace squeezes from the edges of achievement, we discover the difference between a monument to ourselves, and an altar offered to God. Provision flows from purpose because the source isn't our ability; the source is our submission. When you walk in your calling, provision becomes a byproduct rather than the pursuit. Chase money and you will always need more. Seek the King and you will lack no good thing for the assignment He has given you.

This is the clean dividing line for a Kingdom entrepreneur. The world defines prosperity as accumulation. The Kingdom frames prosperity as alignment. When the heart is aligned with God's purpose, resources arrive as tools, not trophies.

Trusting God in The Gaps

Anyone who has followed God into a big assignment knows the reality of gaps. The invoice is late. The estimate was off. The month ran longer than the cash. Gaps aren't evidence of abandonment. They're invitations to intimacy and wisdom.

Elijah learned this in Zarephath. He wasn't sent to a wealthy patron with a stocked pantry. He was sent to a widow who was measuring out her last meal. The supply didn't arrive in a heap. It arrived one scoop at a time. The jar didn't overflow with flour. It simply didn't run out. The mercy was daily, and daily mercy taught a prophet to have a steady ear for God.

The gaps also teach us that trust never cancels stewardship. Budgets are a form of faith because they declare that God works through order, not only through windfalls. Saving isn't doubt; it's wisdom. Negotiation isn't greed; it's stewardship. Building margin isn't fear; it's love for those who depend on our leadership. Faith isn't a substitute for diligence. Faith fuels diligence with courage. We pray over plans and then we plan as if prayer works, because it does.

There will be days when the math doesn't add up and you feel the ache of the unknown. Bring it to God. Bring the balance sheet, too. Ask for wisdom, then make the next right decision. God hasn't changed His name. He's still Jehovah Jireh, your Provider. He doesn't always send more than enough in advance. He often sends enough for today so that you will return to Him tomorrow, because dependence forms the kind of leader He can trust with more.

Provision Looks Like People

Provision doesn't always fall from the sky. Often it knocks on your door wearing work boots or sends a message late at night with an idea you weren't considering. Relationships, mentors, partners, and allies are ordinary channels of God's supply. As Paul said, *"I planted the seed, Apollos watered it, but God has been making it grow."* — *1 Corinthians 3:6.* God loves to wrap provision in people.

I've lived that pattern. After losing a career I valued, I entered a hallway where every door seemed locked. Applications went out. Silence returned. One night, a former coworker sent a text message asking if I would be interested in buying the business where I once worked. My first reply was short: "No!" I didn't want to return to that kind of work.

Two weeks passed, and my wife finally convinced me to at least sit down with the owner. Out of options, I agreed to a meeting.

The owner, nearing retirement, was weighing two paths. He could sell the business whole or liquidate the equipment and shut it down. After we talked, he named a price that sounded unreal until he explained it. $10,000. It was an arbitrary number. His accountant needed a value on the books for tax purposes, and he landed on that figure. That was the exact amount in our savings account. He didn't care if I paid up front, in two parts, or in monthly payments until the $10,000 was paid in full.

The business was debt free, had a strong reputation, and was already booked several weeks out. Even if we failed, the equipment could be sold to recover the money. We shook hands, and the journey began.

Years later, that venture has grown more than 500%. The lesson isn't that faith always delivers a discount or a windfall. The lesson is that God delights to seed His assignments through people, timing, and doors we wouldn't have considered otherwise.

Provision sounded like a late-night text. It looked like humility in an older owner and courage in a younger one. It demanded stewardship, long days, and constant prayer. It also required open eyes to see that God was providing help in the form of people, not only in the form of cash.

Here is the leadership takeaway. Keep your relational radar up. Pray for divine appointments. Protect your reputation so that when opportunity knocks, trust already exists. Ask God for partners whose character runs deeper than their skill. Expect provision to walk into the room.

Redefining Prosperity

Prosperity in the Kingdom isn't the art of gathering more for ourselves. It's the grace of allowing more to flow through us. God's vision for increase is a river, not a reservoir. If revenue rises while generosity sits still, our hearts are drifting toward a smaller kingdom. If the brand grows while compassion shrinks, the soul is starving under the success.

Scripture frames prosperity as purpose-driven. *"But remember the Lord your God, for it is he who gives you the ability to produce wealth."* — *Deuteronomy 8:18*.

The ability to create value is a gift, and gifts come with purpose. When God blesses a business, He has people on His mind. He has employees, apprentices, local families, and global needs on His mind. Wealth becomes a tool to advance His mission, care for people, stabilize households, and seed generosity that outlives us.

This view adjusts our decision-making. We still watch margins, terms, and timelines, yet we also ask questions the world forgets. Who will benefit beyond me if this succeeds? What disciplines will keep my heart soft? What percentage of increase will automatically pass through to others so that my soul doesn't shrink as my capacity grows? When provision is tied to purpose, generosity isn't an afterthought. It's a design principle.

Scripture offers living portraits of God's ability to provide in unlikely ways, and each one anchors the heart of a builder. Picture the wilderness after Egypt. The people woke to a landscape dusted with bread. They gathered what each household needed for the day and discovered that the lesson was larger than food. Manna trained their memory to expect God each morning. It taught them that the Provider cares for bodies and souls, and that hoarding is the enemy of trust.

Think then of a thirsty camp in a barren place. There wasn't a well to dig and no caravan in sight. At God's instruction, Moses struck a rock and water poured from what looked lifeless. The miracle met a physical need, but it also trained a people to stop deciding what is possible by looking only at what is visible. The Source can draw provision from places we would never choose.

Peter was down by the lake. Taxes were due and money was short. Jesus told Peter to cast a line and open the mouth of the first fish he caught. He was confused but still complied. Inside was a coin with the exact value needed. It was a small story, yet it speaks to leaders who worry about details. The King sees details. He knows invoices and deadlines. He can place what you need where you will be, if you will keep following Him.

Finally, imagine a hillside crowd with growling stomachs and no catering plan. A boy offered a lunch meant for one. Jesus took it, blessed it, and the insufficient became abundant. People ate until they were full, and 12 baskets of leftovers told the story that scarcity wasn't going to win. God doesn't need much to do a lot. He looks for surrendered hearts and willing offerings, then He multiplies in ways that feed more than hunger.

None of these moments were predictable. They were responses to obedience. Provision meets motion. As you step into what God has called you to do, He meets you in the middle. Not before, in a way that would cancel faith, not after, in a way that would punish it, but along the path where faith and diligence walk together.

Presence Over Provision

Provision is a promise; it's not the prize. Presence is. Moses knew this when he prayed, *"If your Presence does not go with us, do not send us up from here."* — *Exodus 33:15*.

Moses wanted the Giver more than the gift, the Guide more than the destination, the Presence more than the land itself. That alignment protects every builder. What good is a windfall if peace evaporates? What good is a scaled company if the soul has withered? When presence leads, provision finds its rightful place. When presence is sidelined, provision becomes a trap.

"Seek first his kingdom and his righteousness, and all these things will be given to you as well." — *Matthew 6:33*.

The order matters.

First the Kingdom, then the things.

First the King, then the tools.

First His righteousness shaping our motives, then the needs of our assignment.

It's not a formula to control God. It's an invitation to stay close to Him. When your eyes are fixed on the King, anxiety loosens its grip. You still plan, negotiate, and deliver, but you do so from rest rather than panic. You trust that the One who has written your assignment will fund it in His way and His time.

Here's a practical way to keep presence first. Begin and end the workday with brief, honest prayer. Invite the Spirit to search your motives, to purify your ambition, and to highlight your next step. Keep Sabbath as an act of trust. Tell God in advance how you will use increase, then follow through. Teach your team that excellence is worship, generosity is joy, and integrity is non-negotiable. These rhythms don't earn provision.

If you find yourself in a lean season, don't assume you missed God. It may be the exact place where He is training your ears, strengthening your character for future weight, and arranging a door that will open through a person rather than a spreadsheet. Realign your motives with His Kingdom. Step forward again. Provision will meet you in motion.

For the entrepreneur weighing a new hire, a lease, or a product launch, this principle offers clarity. Start with purpose. Ask which option most clearly aligns with the assignment God has given you. Then move your feet. Expect God to confirm with the right people, the right terms, and the right timing. Don't measure faithfulness by immediate surplus. Measure it by obedience shaped through wisdom.

God isn't stingy; He's generous. He funds purpose, not preference. He sends manna in deserts, water from rock, coins through fish, and capacity through people. He teaches you to budget without losing wonder and to plan without losing dependence. Above all, He walks with you. That presence is the true wealth of a builder. Seek Him first, and you will not lack what you need to do what He has called you to do. That's the rhythm of Kingdom provision. Purpose first, then everything else. Provision follows purpose. Always.

WALK IT OUT

Trusting God's Flow

To trust God's flow is to rest in the truth that provision always follows purpose. When you build what He has called you to build, He supplies what's needed in His perfect time. Begin by replacing fear with faith in your financial thinking. Stop asking, "Do I have enough?" and start asking, "Am I aligned with what God asked me to do?" Alignment attracts provision. When your work matches His will, resource flows like a river that never runs dry.

Start every financial decision with prayer. Before you sign, spend, or start something new, invite God into the process. Ask Him to confirm what carries His blessing and to block what isn't meant for you. This posture doesn't make you passive; it keeps you protected. Divine flow begins with divine direction.

Practice generosity even when you feel stretched. Giving keeps your heart anchored in trust. It reminds you that you're a steward, not an owner, and that what flows through your hands can never run out as long as it stays connected to His source. Track your gratitude as closely as your income. Each answered prayer, each unexpected provision, each small win becomes proof that He provides faithfully.

When worry rises, worship instead. Speak God's promises out loud until peace returns. The moment you shift from striving to surrender, you'll feel the current of His provision catch you again. Trusting God's flow isn't about avoiding work or waiting idly; it's about working from rest and knowing that He multiplies what He authors. God funds every faithful assignment, and peace becomes the currency you live by.

CHAPTER TEN

Anointed to Build

A Blueprint for Kingdom Legacy.

"I am carrying on a great project and cannot go down." — *Nehemiah 6:3*

Jerusalem's walls were in ruins, a city exposed, a people defeated. Yet from the luxury of a Persian palace, Nehemiah felt the weight of a divine burden. He didn't just see rubble; he saw a calling. He left comfort to restore legacy. His powerful declaration in the face of relentless opposition, "I am carrying on a great project and cannot go down," isn't just a historical footnote. It's the rally cry for every person who feels called to create something of eternal significance.

Nehemiah understood that a God-given vision requires a persistent spirit, and that true builders are defined not by the size of the project but by their unwavering commitment to finish it, no matter the cost or the criticism. This principle of sustained obedience is the very heartbeat of a life lived for the Kingdom.

The Builder's Calling

You weren't created merely to work; you were anointed to build a legacy. There's a sacred distinction. Work pays bills. Building leaves a legacy. Work fills time. Building fulfills purpose. In the Kingdom, there's a difference between making a living and living out your calling. God didn't design you for survival; He anointed you for construction. You're here to establish something that carries Heaven's fingerprints, to leave a mark on the world that points back to God.

From the beginning, God revealed Himself as a builder. In Genesis, the first picture we get of God isn't a preacher or a warrior, but a

Creator. He shapes the cosmos with rhythm, order, and intention. Then He forms humanity and gives them the blueprint: be fruitful, multiply, subdue, cultivate, and steward. This wasn't just about farming. It was about expanding His order into the earth, bringing His design into every corner of the world. Eden was the prototype. Humanity was commissioned to extend it.

This wasn't just Eden's mandate; it's ours too. God still calls His people to extend His Kingdom through craftsmanship, leadership, and innovation.

We are co-creators with God, invited to participate in the ongoing work of making His world whole again. Consider the software developer who designs an app that connects people with local food banks. They're not just writing code; they're participating in God's design for community and provision. Or the entrepreneur who builds a company based on ethical supply chains, giving dignity to workers around the globe. They're not just creating a product; they're extending God's justice into the marketplace. This is what it means to be a co-creator, to see every act of construction, no matter how small, as a sacred act of divine partnership.

Jesus continued the pattern. Before He preached, He built. Before He called disciples, He shaped wood. The Savior of the world was a carpenter by trade. That wasn't filler; it was formation. Years of craftsmanship trained His hands in precision, patience, and unseen progress. His earthly ministry was short, however His years as a builder laid the foundation of character and diligence that would define His public life.

What you build in obscurity prepares you for the influence you haven't yet seen. It's in the quiet, mundane moments of faithfulness that your true authority is forged. The humility of the carpenter prepares the heart of the King.

When you build with Kingdom purpose, your work becomes

worship. Whether you're designing code, raising children, launching a nonprofit, or repairing HVAC units. You're not just completing tasks. You're establishing something eternal, a tangible expression of your faith in action. God doesn't just anoint sermons; He anoints systems, spreadsheets, structures, and blueprints. He is as glorified by the careful execution of a business plan as He is by a powerful prophetic word.

Every hammer swing. Every late night. Every spreadsheet revision. Every staff meeting. When done in obedience and excellence, it becomes part of your worship, an offering to the One who gave you the vision. Building isn't a distraction from your calling. It's your calling.

What Are You Building?

Everyone is building something. The question is: what is your foundation? Some build platforms. Some build wealth. Others build image, but Kingdom builders construct what reflects Heaven and serves people beyond themselves. They build on a foundation of eternal values, not temporary gains.

Are you building something that God assigned, or something your ego initiated? One leads to purpose and peace. The other leads to burnout and a hollow kind of success. It's easy to confuse momentum for mission. Just because something grows doesn't mean it's from God. Just because a door is open doesn't mean it leads to obedience.

Not all building is bad, but not all building is blessed. The difference lies in the blueprint.

Kingdom builders know this. They don't chase every opportunity. They follow blueprints from Heaven, understanding that divine strategy is far more reliable than human hustle.

I've watched leaders build what I call "vanity projects": things that look incredible from the outside but are built on the shifting sand of ego. They get momentum, they gain followers, and they're showered with praise. Then, after a few years, they burn out, the foundation crumbles, and the hollow nature of their work is exposed. They discovered too late that momentum isn't a substitute for mission, and popularity can't fill the hole in your purpose.

A Kingdom builder knows the difference between a project that satisfies the soul and a project that merely inflates the self.

The Wall Is Worth It

Nehemiah wasn't a builder by profession. He was a cupbearer to the king, a servant with access to royalty but no résumé in construction. Yet God called him to rebuild the broken walls of Jerusalem. He stepped into an assignment he wasn't professionally qualified for but spiritually equipped for.

As he built, opposition rose. Critics mocked him. Enemies plotted. Distractions increased. Yet, Nehemiah's focus never wavered. When asked to come down from the wall and meet with his enemies, his response was legendary: *"I am doing a great work, and I cannot come down."*

That is the heart of a Kingdom builder.

Similarly, TV personality Mike Rowe built his brand not on a product but on a purpose. Through his popular television show Dirty Jobs™, he was introduced to a forgotten part of the American workforce. He saw the dignity and pride of men and women who quietly keep the world running, and he carried a burden to close the gap between millions of available jobs and a culture that had begun to devalue skilled labor. Out of that conviction, he launched the mikeroweWORKS Foundation™, which has given millions of dollars in scholarships to people pursuing careers in the trades.

Mike's work challenges the idea that success is measured only by a four-year degree. He actively promotes what he calls the S.W.E.A.T. Pledge™ (Skills and Work Ethic Aren't Taboo). This pledge outlines a set of core beliefs about personal responsibility and hard work, and he invites people to build their lives on that foundation. For Mike, it's more than a clever slogan. It's a blueprint for building a meaningful life. His business and charitable efforts are not about chasing profit or building a platform; they're about reshaping how society values work and about serving those who are often overlooked.

You will face resistance. If what you're building is from God, it will threaten the comfort of those who've settled. It will disturb darkness. Of course, darkness always pushes back when light starts to rise. Expect it. Don't be surprised when critics show up. Don't panic when your progress gets interrupted, and don't trade your wall for a meeting with people who don't understand your assignment. Stay on the wall, because the work you're doing is far more important than the opinions of those who only stand by and watch.

Distractions or Opportunities

Not every opportunity is from God. Some of the most dangerous detours are wrapped in compliments and offers. It might look like a promotion, a partnership, or even a ministry door, but if it pulls you away from your assignment, it's not elevation; it's erosion.

Distraction isn't always sinful. Sometimes it's subtle. A new business venture. A viral trend. A chance to impress. A relationship that seems helpful but drains your spiritual clarity. These things don't announce themselves as opposition. They just slowly bleed your focus, energy, and resources until you're no longer making progress on the things that truly matter.

Many are derailed not by sin, but by significance, the illusion of it, anyway.

Nehemiah's enemies tried to trick him with diplomacy. "Let's talk. Let's collaborate. Let's meet." He discerned the motive. Nehemiah's opposition wasn't a simple disagreement; it was a sophisticated, political plot. His enemies tried to lure him to a place called Ono, pretending to want a meeting of diplomacy. Nehemiah discerned their motive: they wanted to ambush and harm him.

His response was a masterpiece of focus. He didn't waste time negotiating or explaining. He simply sent messengers with the famous reply: *"I am carrying on a great project and cannot go down."*

He refused to be distracted by a low-level conflict when he was on a high-level assignment. This is a lesson for every modern builder: discernment is as important as diligence, and your greatest act of obedience may be to say no to what others believe is a good idea.

Protect your wall. Discern the motive. Guard your time, your heart, and your calendar like it matters, because it does.

The Blueprint Requires a Builder

God gives the vision, but He expects you to build. Noah had to construct the ark. Moses had to lead the people. Solomon had to oversee the temple. It's not enough to dream. You must design. It's not enough to get a prophetic word. You need a production plan.

God isn't anti-structure or anti-strategy. Heaven has order. The Kingdom has architecture. Angels are arranged in ranks, and creation is tuned like a symphony. When God assigns you to build, He expects stewardship and execution.

Faith doesn't wait for the clouds to clear. It builds while the sky is still gray.

When God gave Moses the blueprint for the tabernacle, He didn't just create the structure out of thin air. He called on skilled artisans, people with anointed hands and willing hearts, to work.

In the same way, when you receive a divine vision, your faith is what motivates you to draw up a business plan, create a budget, hire the right people, and lay the first brick.

This is the sacred dance of faith and works: God provides the vision, and we provide the obedience, hard work, and stewardship necessary to bring that vision to life.

The Culture You Build

You're not just building products; you're building people. Your business, your team, your household. It has a culture. What you tolerate becomes culture. What you prioritize becomes culture. What you overlook becomes culture.

Culture isn't a mission statement. It's a living ecosystem.

It's how your team feels when you walk in. It's what happens when no one's watching. It's the real values under the surface.

If you're a Kingdom builder, culture must reflect the King. Justice. Honor. Humility. Truth. Excellence. Peace. These aren't decorations. They're foundations. Build systems that foster rest, not burnout. Lead in a way that cultivates growth, not fear. Your culture will outlast your content, and it will be the truest legacy you leave behind.

After a deep conversation with God, I felt Him give me a new direction to develop our culture. I made the shift from construction company operator to leader focus. Today, I look at my company as one that is reshaping men into leaders, redirecting a flawed market mindset from money over value to value driven, and helping to re-establish God as our prioritized go-to expert.

That's not just leadership. That's Kingdom culture made visible.

Stewardship Unlocks Scale

God won't grow what you won't manage. We often ask Him to expand our territory, but we don't steward the square feet we've got. Stewardship is spiritual. It's not just about money. It's how you treat people. How you manage time. How you show up when no one's watching.

Joseph wasn't just a dreamer; he was a manager. He turned famine into a strategy. His leadership saved nations. God gives vision to those who can carry the weight of execution.

Excellence isn't legalism. It's love. It's honoring the people you serve and the God you represent. Build with care. Design with intention. Follow through with precision. This is the path to divine multiplication.

The Parable of the Three Builders

One morning company CEO, John Sill decides to visit one of the company's newest construction sites. As John makes his rounds he stops to chat with a 3 of the workers who were on a quick break. After a short period of introduction, John asks the workers if they'd be honest and answer a simple question. Without hesitation they each agreed. "What are you doing?" John asked.

The first worker said, "Laying bricks."

The second, "Building a wall."

The third pauses for a moment, appearing to contemplate the question a bit more, then says, "Sir, while my partners are right, I feel we're building much more. We're crafting a space where generations will come to worship. Every brick we lay, every screw we tighten, they each matter. They're the totality of a greater vision."

All three were doing the same task, but only one had vision.

You can build emails, or you can build encounters. You can design processes, or you can design environments for peace and restoration.

Kingdom builders see the mission inside the mundane. They don't need applause. They need purpose.

What You Build Must Outlive You

A wise builder thinks generationally. They ask, "Will this last after I'm gone?" Paul didn't just plant churches; he raised leaders. Jesus didn't just preach sermons; He made disciples. The greatest Kingdom builders aren't those who do the most, but those who empower others to do even more.

Your success isn't in what you achieve. It's in what remains when you're gone.

Build with your children in mind. Build with your successors in mind. Build with eternity in mind. You're not the end; you're the vessel. Let your ceiling become someone else's floor.

Stay on the Wall

You will be tempted to come down. There will be days when it feels like no one sees. Like the wall is too big. Like the critics are too loud. Don't stop!

The wall is worth it. The vision is worth it. The people depending on you, those you may never even meet, are worth it.

Nehemiah didn't come down. Not for applause. Not for diplomacy. Not for fear.

Neither should you.

Stay faithful. Keep building. One brick at a time. Because what you build in obedience will outlast what others build in ambition.

CHAPTER TEN

It will stand because the foundation isn't sand, but rock.

WALK IT OUT

Building Under The Anointing

To build under the anointing is to rely on more than your own ability. Skill builds the frame, but the Spirit fills it with life. Every Kingdom builder must learn to depend on divine partnership rather than personal performance. Begin each project, meeting, or task by inviting the Holy Spirit to lead. Pray, "Lord, breathe on this work. Let it carry Your purpose and presence." That prayer transforms ordinary planning into sacred preparation.

Keep your heart pure while you build. The anointing flows through clean hands and a surrendered spirit. Guard against pride when success comes and against doubt when results seem slow. Stay focused on pleasing God rather than impressing people. The anointing is not earned through effort; it's sustained through intimacy. Spend time in His presence daily, even when deadlines feel tight. His presence will reveal solutions no strategy could find.

Honor excellence while remaining sensitive to His voice. Do your work with diligence, but never at the cost of dependence. Ask God to show you when to act, when to pause, and when to let Him work beyond what you can see. When your decisions are guided by His whisper, the results carry His weight.

Building under the anointing means knowing that your greatest strength is submission. The moment you stop relying on your own power, you make room for His. Over time, you'll begin to see that what succeeds isn't just well built—it's divinely breathed. Your labor becomes worship, your leadership becomes ministry, and your results become testimony. That's the mark of an anointed builder: skill directed by the Spirit, creating something that will outlast you because it carries His touch.

CHAPTER ELEVEN
Warfare in the Work

Kingdom ground is always contested ground.

"For our struggle is not against flesh and blood, but against the rulers, against the authorities, against the powers of this dark world and against the spiritual forces of evil in the heavenly realms." — Ephesians 6:12

Kingdom work is not neutral ground. The moment you step into your God-given assignment, you step onto a battlefield. It's not one marked by bombs or bullets, but by spiritual interference. You will face subtle sabotage, invisible resistance, and unseen warfare. Still, so many leaders are caught off guard by it. They begin a business God told them to build or pursue a calling that aligns with Heaven's agenda, only to be met with delay, distraction, disunity, or emotional burnout. They assume something must be wrong, that they have lost their anointing or missed God's voice. Scripture tells us plainly, however, that we wrestle not against flesh and blood.

Your battle is not ultimately against that one-star review or that difficult employee. It's not against rising costs, broken equipment, delayed permits, or competitors who cut corners. Those are the visible symptoms. They're the dust kicked up from the real war happening behind the scenes. This battle is being fought in the quiet moments, when discouragement creeps in, when doubt begins to whisper, and when the ease of quitting seems more appealing than the pain of continuing. The adversary's goal is to make you believe the struggle is merely a logistical or relational problem so that you exhaust your energy solving surface issues while the spiritual roots of the opposition remain untouched.

We don't often talk about spiritual warfare in the marketplace. We should. Every God-ordained assignment will face God-opposing resistance. If you're unaware of the battlefield, you'll misinterpret the fight. You'll start swinging at people instead of principalities. You'll exhaust your strength solving surface problems while ignoring the spiritual root. The enemy's goal is simple: to derail the builder before the wall is finished, to discourage the faithful before the breakthrough comes, and to distract the anointed before they multiply. This is the truth of Kingdom work, a reality few are prepared for. You must recognize the battle and then learn to fight with the right weapons.

Discouragement as a Strategy

R.G. LeTourneau was one of the most innovative Christian industrialists of the twentieth century. He was the founder of LeTourneau Technologies, an earthmoving and heavy-equipment company that helped reshape modern construction. His company supplied three-fourths of the heavy machinery used by the Allied forces during World War II, a significant contribution that helped secure a victory.

From the earliest days of his business, LeTourneau faced a relentless campaign of skepticism and mockery. The industrial world, financiers, and even some fellow believers declared his vision unrealistic. They called his machines impractical, his giving habits foolish, and his insistence on running a company dedicated to God naïve. Rumors spread that he was on the verge of bankruptcy, that his ideas would never work, and that faith had no place in manufacturing. The attack wasn't sabotage; it was quieter and more corrosive. It was the constant whisper that building with conviction in the marketplace was impossible.

The discouragement nearly worked. There were seasons when LeTourneau's factories sat silent, contracts collapsed, and creditors circled. Many assumed he would give up and close his doors. He refused. Instead, he placed his trust in God, invested what little remained, and told his team that if God had called them to build, He would make a way. His perseverance, even when every sign pointed toward failure, eventually transformed his small machine shop into one of the most influential industrial companies in the world.

When LeTourneau sold the business in 1953 for $31 million, equivalent to roughly $375 million in today's value, it stood as proof that faith-fueled persistence can reshape both industries and destinies. He lived out a truth every Kingdom builder must hold onto: opposition is often the clearest sign that what you're building truly matters.

As you see, discouragement doesn't only show up in boardrooms and headlines. It can creep into our own teams, our families, and even the people sitting right next to us. I learned this lesson myself, firsthand.

One of my own team members had become increasingly discouraged in just about all aspects of their job. They're an exceptional team member, and I was committed to getting to the root of the issue.

We met and had an extended, in-depth conversation. I asked if there was anything I could improve or if there was anything about the work environment that was frustrating them. To my surprise, they told me it had nothing to do with me or the job. They confessed that they were struggling mentally, a battle that went back to their childhood. As we talked more, they mentioned they lived alone and were introverted, which meant they had little to no interaction with others outside of work.

Bingo. The answer had been there all along, but I had never simply asked. I had assumed the problem was job-related. I missed the deeper opportunity. It broke my heart and I immediately realized I was not being Kingdom-focused enough. Yes, I was always concerned with their job going smoothly so they could reclaim their time, but I had missed a chance to ask about the heart. Sometimes, that's all it takes.

A simple conversation can shift everything, boosting morale and affirming the sacred worth of the person in front of you.

The Lord strengthens those who stay the course. Courage, in the Kingdom, is not about personality or loud declarations. It's about quiet persistence. It's about picking up your tools the next morning after a hard day, praying through the ache, and choosing to believe that what you're building is worth the resistance. Every nail driven, every hour given, every prayer lifted. It all matters. Courage does not wait for ideal conditions. It keeps building in the storm.

Fighting From Victory, Not for It

Many believers approach spiritual warfare from a posture of panic. They feel as if the outcome is still undecided, as if the burden of breakthrough rests entirely on their shoulders. The gospel changes everything. Jesus already won the victory. *"He disarmed the rulers and authorities and made a public spectacle of them, triumphing over them by the cross"*— *Colossians 2:15*. This means we fight not for victory, but from it. That is a crucial distinction that shifts our perspective from desperation to confidence. It empowers us to be still and know that He is God, even when the enemy's noise is at its loudest.

This is why spiritual disciplines aren't religious accessories for the Christian entrepreneur. They're essential armor. Prayer is your communication line to headquarters. When the lies of the enemy begin to take root, prayer is your way of calling for divine backup. Worship is a weapon that shifts the climate around you, silences the noise of the world with the truth of God's character. Scripture trains your thinking and anchors your decisions, helping you discern between a God-inspired idea and an enemy-inspired thought. Community becomes your shield when your arms are tired.

When the pressure rises, the temptation will be to hustle harder.

To work longer. To carry the whole load yourself. Kingdom builders know better. When others power through, we power down, because that's where strength is truly found. You retreat so you can return, not broken and burned out, but refilled and recommissioned for the battle.

Protecting Your Mind and Mission

The most brutal war is often waged between your ears. You know the pattern. One negative comment or an unexpected delay, and suddenly you question your worth. The lies don't scream; they whisper: "You're not qualified." "No one cares." "This isn't working." Left unchecked, those thoughts don't just sabotage your day. They sabotage your destiny.

Scripture says to take every thought captive. Your mind is not a passive battlefield; it's your command center. If the enemy can plant lies there, he can paralyze your decisions. He doesn't need your body. He just needs your agreement. When a lie whispers, "This isn't working," you take that thought captive by speaking truth: "I'm building what God called me to build, and His work always prospers."

If he wins your thoughts, he steers your direction. So, fight back. Don't let the enemy narrate your story. Speak life. Fill your space with worship that declares the truth of who God is. Saturate your routine with prayer, praise, and purpose. Surround yourself with people who see the vision and remind you of it when you forget.

You're not just defending your business; you're defending your calling. Your calling is worth protecting. That contract is not just income. That product is not just a SKU. That team member is not just labor. Every piece of what you build carries spiritual significance. Guard it accordingly.

The Power of Perseverance

We tend to think of warfare in terms of big spiritual showdowns: dramatic moments, powerful prayers, mountain-moving miracles. However, some of the most powerful spiritual acts are deceptively ordinary. The email you send when you're exhausted. The conversation you show up for when you would rather hide. The prayer whispered in traffic. The lunch break where you pause to ask God for help. They're the moments that declare to the spiritual realm that you will not give up.

Perseverance is prophetic. It speaks into the spiritual realm and declares, "I believe what God said, even when nothing around me looks like it." The world applauds speed and spectacle. Heaven applauds faithfulness. It doesn't care how flashy the launch was; it's watching to see if you'll still be there when no one else is. It's watching to see if you'll pick up the hammer again after disappointment.

The termination I mentioned earlier was a crushing blow that pushed me into a spiral of depression and frustration. The enemy's whispers were loud and constant. However, I refused to stay in that place. I connected with others, a small circle of trusted friends and mentors, who spoke life over me. They and my family reminded me of my value outside of my job title. Through their support and a commitment to seeking God daily, I slowly started to overcome. What pulled me through was not just grit. It was grace.

Healing from that experience was not a quick process; it was an extended, yet powerful one, filled with small, ordinary acts of perseverance. I had to choose every day to pick myself back up and believe in my God-given purpose. This journey of overcoming led me to a new level of clarity and a deeper understanding of what it means to build with faith, even when the world is telling you to quit.

Build and Battle

The business you're building may look like numbers, logistics, and client meetings on the outside. However, on the inside, it's a spiritual assignment. It's a light on a hill. It's a fortress of integrity in a culture of compromise. Because of that, it will be opposed. Don't mistake opposition for failure. Sometimes, it's the clearest sign you're on the right track.

You must stay at your post. Keep your eyes focused and your ears open. Remember this: the warfare is temporary, but the fruit is eternal. The fight may feel long, but the victory is already yours.

WALK IT OUT

Standing Firm While Building

Every Kingdom assignment attracts opposition. The closer you get to completion, the louder the enemy becomes. This is not a sign that you've missed God's will; it's evidence that you're carrying something valuable. Begin by deciding that opposition will not define your outcome. You can't always control the storm, but you can choose your stance within it.

Start your mornings by declaring peace over your day. Invite the Holy Spirit to guard your thoughts before chaos has a chance to enter. When discouragement whispers that you're falling behind, remember that the goal isn't speed but stability. God's favor rests on those who remain faithful even when progress feels slow.

Keep your worship active while you work. Play praise music while you prepare, pray as you plan, and speak God's promises as you perform your tasks. Worship builds a wall around your mind that keeps fear from gaining ground. When anxiety tries to distract you, respond with gratitude. Thank God for the privilege of building with Him. Gratitude will silence the noise of worry every time.

Surround yourself with people who remind you of what God said when you feel weary. Isolation feeds fear, while agreement fuels faith. Let trusted voices pray with you, encourage you, and stand beside you until the breakthrough comes. When you keep your hands on the work and your heart anchored in worship, you'll discover that the very battles meant to break you become the tools God uses to strengthen you.

CHAPTER TWELVE
Don't Build Alone

The Power of Kingdom Collaborations.

"Two are better than one, because they have a good return for their labor." — Ecclesiastes 4:9

The world idolizes the lone visionary, the self-made entrepreneur grinding in isolation, fueled by ambition, blazing a trail no one else could follow. It's a compelling story, one we've all been told in movies, podcasts, and bestsellers. It's a seductive tale of fierce independence and personal triumph against all odds. That is a dangerous narrative, and it's certainly not a Kingdom story. It's a myth that, while inspiring on the surface, often leads to burnout and brokenness behind the scenes. The reality of this myth is a heavy burden, a crushing weight that no single person was ever designed to carry.

This isn't about chasing visibility; it's about shared responsibility. Collaboration isn't a stage strategy; it's a spiritual safeguard. Where **Chapter Five: Vision Over Virality** challenged the motives behind what we build, this chapter reveals the power found in who we build with.

Few modern figures embody this myth more than Steve Jobs. He is often remembered as the lone wolf, the genius who built Apple through sheer force of will. The truth, however, tells a different story. He was not a lone builder. He was a master collaborator who knew how to surround himself with people whose skills and perspectives he lacked. As Jobs himself put it, "Great things in business are never done by one person. They're done by a team of people."

Apple's foundation rested on Steve Wozniak's engineering brilliance, which turned vision into reality. Years later, when he returned to Apple, Jobs's partnership with Jony Ive drove the company's resurgence, blending vision and design into products that reshaped culture. He may have been the face of the company, but he was never building alone.

That truth runs deeper than business. From the very beginning, God declared a principle that challenges the myth of the lone builder: *"It is not good for man to be alone."* — *Genesis 2:18*. This was not just a comment on marriage; it was a foundational blueprint for human existence, for mission, for work, and for life itself. We were created to walk with others, to co-labor, and to carry vision in community. This principle did not die in Eden; it was re-established and amplified throughout all of Scripture. It still defines how we're called to build in leadership, business, and every area of Kingdom purpose. To ignore this principle is to build on a flawed foundation that will eventually crack under the pressure of isolation.

We see this truth woven throughout Scripture in countless examples. Paul, one of the most influential church planters in history, did not travel solo on his missionary journeys. He was consistently surrounded by a dynamic team that included Timothy, Silas, Luke, Barnabas, Priscilla, and Aquila. Each person brought a different gift, a unique perspective, and a specific anointing to the mission. Together, they covered more ground, built stronger churches, and faced greater opposition than Paul ever could have alone.

Even Jesus, fully divine and lacking nothing, sent His disciples out two by two. He could have accomplished the mission alone in a single act of divine power, but He chose to model the foundational truth of how the Kingdom advances: not through individual heroics, but through partnership, unity, and shared vulnerability.

Isolation might look impressive on a highlight reel or in a self-help book, but it shatters under the weight of real-world pressure. You were never meant to carry the full weight of a God-sized vision alone. In fact, trying to do so is often a subtle, and sometimes not so subtle, sign of pride.

I know this from experience. Like many leaders, I once clung to the lone-wolf mentality, convincing myself that I was the only one who could truly steer the ship. My greatest fear was relinquishing control of "my baby," the business God had entrusted to me. I thought that if I shared the vision too openly, someone would eventually take it in a different direction. I held on to that belief until I reached a point of exhaustion. I was worn down, burned out, and completely overwhelmed. I was trying to be the CEO, creative lead, salesperson, and visionary all at once.

It was in that season of depletion that I finally asked myself: if I have spent all this time training and equipping my team, shouldn't I be able to trust them with the direction now? If not, what was the point of their presence? That question became a turning point. It lifted a weight I was never meant to carry and began reclaiming time, energy, and mental clarity. The most surprising part was that the business grew faster than it ever had before. I didn't lose control. I redirected it appropriately and with peace. I moved from doing all the work to guiding the work, from guarding the vision to sharing it.

This is what God intended, a body working together, each part fulfilling its purpose for the good of the whole. This is how we defeat the myth of the lone builder. Kingdom assignments are built shoulder to shoulder, in humility and service, not platform to platform in competition and ego.

Why Collaboration Builds Stronger

Collaboration is far more than a leadership strategy. It's a spiritual principle. Scripture doesn't whisper this truth. It declares it boldly: *"Two are better than one, because they have a good return for their labor." — Ecclesiastes 4:9.*

This verse speaks of divine return, a supernatural multiplication that solo efforts cannot match. When we work in unity with the Spirit, our combined impact becomes exponentially greater than what we could accomplish alone. This is the economy of the Kingdom, operating on generosity, trust, and shared labor.

My pastor once defined fellowship as "two fellows in the same ship." It's simple, but profound. It reminds us we're all navigating life's waters, and that journey isn't meant to be sailed alone. We need mentors, confidants, and co-builders, even if they're not directly involved in our business or ministry. We need someone to help us course-correct. We don't have all the ideas, and we certainly don't have all the best ones.

When you build alongside others who carry the same Spirit and share a Kingdom mandate, your mission expands beyond your natural limits. You no longer bear the burden alone, and that freedom enables you to fully operate in your anointing. You gain a new vantage point. What you miss, they catch. You dream bigger because creativity blooms in communion. You also endure longer. When your strength fades, their faith can carry you through. That's the power of Kingdom unity. One falters, the other lifts. One forgets the vision, the other reminds. One grows weary, the other intercedes. The enemy knows this, which is why his top strategy is division.

Healthy Partnerships

In a world obsessed with competition and personal brand, we must recover the sacred value of partnership. Social media makes it easy to compare and feel threatened by someone else's breakthrough. However, in the Kingdom, someone else's win doesn't jeopardize yours. It confirms it. When God is moving in their life, it's a sign that He's moving in yours too. The tide is rising, and we all rise with it.

Personally, I don't view other businesses as competition. Some offer similar services, but they don't control my outcomes. My success is determined by how I steward what God has entrusted to me; how I treat my team, my clients, and my calling. Strong competitors sharpen us. They push us toward excellence. If we pay attention, we can learn from their success. This mindset removes rivalry and replaces it with refinement. We don't tear each other down. We grow together.

True partnership goes deeper than shared vision. It's about mutual submission. It's not built on convenience or self-interest, but on trust, accountability, and sacrifice. When you build with someone who shares your heart, not just your goal, you unlock a divine alignment that no algorithm or business model can replicate.

It looks like celebrating their wins like they're your own, giving your time and influence without fear, and saying the hard truth in love. Most importantly, it means keeping your focus on God's glory, not your platform. These are spiritual partnerships, not transactions. Forged in humility and anchored in trust, they reflect the heart of God. When the goal is His glory and the advancement of His Kingdom, there's no room for rivalry, only mutual refinement.

Discerning Kingdom Partnerships

Let's be clear. Not every partnership is from God. Some will drain you. Others will distract or even derail your calling. This is why discernment must outweigh opportunity. The world offers opportunities. The Kingdom offers divine assignments.

Before you link arms with someone, link hearts with God. Ask Him to reveal their fruit, not just their flair. Is this person aligned with your values? Are they submitted to Christ or only to their ambition? Are they building for the Kingdom or for clout?

A wrong partnership may share your vision but not your heart.

They may agree with your mission but resist your submission to God. They may be wildly gifted but spiritually misaligned. Consider Paul and Barnabas in *Acts 15*. These faithful missionaries had a sharp disagreement about John Mark. Barnabas wanted to give him another chance. Paul didn't. The dispute led them to part ways. It wasn't about theology. It was about strategy.

While painful, their separation ultimately resulted in two missionary teams instead of one. Even Spirit-filled leaders sometimes need to walk in different directions. The key is knowing when to stay and when to release.

So how do you spot the right kind of partner? Look for humility, not self-promotion. For people who speak life into your purpose, not suspicion. For those who build quietly and faithfully when no one is watching. Most importantly, see how they respond when things get hard. True covenant partners don't run when it's costly. They dig in deeper and lock shields with you.

Collaboration Reflects the Heart of God

From the beginning, God modeled collaboration in Himself. The Trinity isn't a strategic shortcut. It's the divine blueprint. Father, Son, and Holy Spirit operate in unbroken unity. Each glorifies the other. Each submits in love. Each fulfills a role in the redemptive story.

Jesus said, *"I do nothing on my own but speak just what the Father has taught me." —John 8:28.*

That's not a statement of limitation. It's a declaration of perfect alignment.

When we build in partnership, Spirit-led, mission-focused, and ego-free, we reflect that same divine image. Our unity becomes a witness. Our collaboration becomes an altar. It shows the world a different way to build, one that doesn't devour or divide, but blesses and multiplies.

Lasting Words

So, who's building with you?

Who reminds you of the vision when fatigue sets in? Who holds up your arms when the warfare hits? Who rejoices when you win and grieves when you suffer? Who tells you the truth when you drift?

You were never meant to build alone, and you don't have to.

Pray for the right people. Not just the gifted, but the surrendered. Not just the capable, but the committed. Invite them in. Honor them when they come. Celebrate their presence. Protect their hearts.

We don't build to be seen; we build to be strengthened. Collaboration guards the mission from pride and isolation the same way humility guards the heart from performance. When our focus shifts from being noticed to being knit together, Kingdom work endures.

The Kingdom won't be built by hustlers chasing influence. It'll be built by a remnant of united builders. These are leaders submitted to Christ, steady in purpose, and shoulder to shoulder. They're not driven by ambition but rooted in alignment and empowered by His presence.

WALK IT OUT

Building Together

To build together is to recognize that Kingdom success was never meant to be a solo project. God advances His purposes through collaboration, not competition. Begin by asking Him to show you who belongs in your circle for this season. Pray specifically for divine partnerships—people whose character aligns with your calling and whose strengths complement your own. Unity is powerful when it's intentional.

Value relationships more than recognition. When others succeed, celebrate them sincerely. The more you honor what God is doing through others, the more freely He moves through you. Healthy builders lift each other. Jealousy divides, but humility multiplies. Make it your aim to add value wherever you serve, even when your contribution is unseen.

Keep communication open and clear. Misunderstanding weakens momentum, so speak truthfully, listen patiently, and lead with grace. Protect the trust that partnership requires. When conflict arises, address it quickly. Forgive easily. The unity you fight to preserve today will protect the fruit you enjoy tomorrow.

Learn to share both the weight and the wins. Delegation isn't loss of control; it's proof of maturity. Give others the opportunity to shine and to steward their own assignments. When each person carries their portion with excellence, the collective effort becomes a reflection of God's order.

Building together is how heaven's architecture takes shape on earth. Alone you can create something good, but together you can create something eternal. Choose connection over isolation, cooperation over ego, and love over pride. The Kingdom always grows faster when its builders link arms rather than build walls.

CHAPTER THIRTEEN
Legacy Over Likes

Torchbearers Over Trendsetters.

"One generation commends your works to another; they tell of your mighty acts." — Psalm 145:4

The world measures success in followers, likes, and trending moments. It's a fast-moving, noisy system that rewards what's popular right now. However, as a Kingdom builder, you were never called to go viral. You were called to build what lasts. The Kingdom doesn't celebrate momentary fame or the fleeting attention of a crowd; it honors faithfulness, obedience, and fruit that remains long after the applause fades.

Legacy isn't about your personal brand or the size of your platform. It's about the people you impact and the foundations you lay long after your name is forgotten. It's about building something so solid, so anchored in truth, that it continues to bear fruit for generations to come.

This principle is seen most profoundly in the life of Jesus. He spent most of His ministry not addressing large crowds but investing deeply in just twelve people. There was no social media strategy, no marketing team, and no effort to "go viral." Yet His legacy is the one that transformed eternity itself.

The question for us today isn't about how big your platform is or how many people know your name. The real question is: what kind of fruit will still be standing generations from now because you chose faithfulness over fame? Will your work be a monument to yourself, or a living, breathing testament to the God you serve?

Legacy is about the unseen moments. It's about the prayers whispered over your children when no one is around. It's about the conversations you have with your team when you're choosing values over shortcuts. It's about the nights you stay up interceding for someone who may never even know you prayed. These are the investments that outlast fame, because they're sown in eternity. While the world shouts, "Be known now," the Spirit whispers, "Be faithful forever." The beauty of legacy is that it multiplies even when no one is counting, because Heaven keeps score differently. What looks small here will be monumental in eternity.

Likes Feed Ego, Legacy Feeds Generations

It's incredibly easy to be seduced by applause. Metrics and analytics make us feel validated and successful. A growing number of followers or a spike in engagement can feel like a direct affirmation of our work. However, when our work is fueled by external approval, we're constantly trading depth for visibility. The world tells you that if you're not seen, you don't matter. Which is a lie.

You can go viral and still be spiritually bankrupt. You can be popular and still miss your purpose entirely. You can be praised by the world and still unknown in Heaven.

Obedience in the Kingdom often looks like obscurity. Still, some of the most impactful, world-changing Kingdom work is done in rooms that never trend and in fields that never get photographed. This is the work that God honors, because it's done for an audience of One.

Chasing likes is like trying to build a permanent structure on shifting sand. It's shallow, unstable, and subject to the unpredictable winds of public opinion. Legacy, on the other hand, is what happens when you commit to building your life on the Rock, which is Christ Jesus. It's the result of serving without needing recognition. It's the quiet discipline of discipling a few instead of trying to entertain the many. It's the long-term vision of investing in the next generation instead of competing with them for influence.

This kind of work isn't glamorous. However, it's deeply fruitful. It's the difference between building a reputation that can be torn down tomorrow and building a character that will stand for all time.

Legacy of a Torchbearer

Torchbearers don't live for the fleeting glory of the flame. They live to pass it on to the next runner in the race. Paul didn't spend his life building a personal platform; he spent it building people. He poured his life, his wisdom, and his anointing into Timothy, not because Timothy would praise him or increase his influence, but because the Gospel had to keep moving. The mission was bigger than his life. True legacy isn't about maintenance; it's about multiplication. It's about what continues without you, not what centers around you. It's about a vision that's so compelling, so anointed, that it can be carried forward by others long after you're gone.

You were never meant to be the hero of the story. You're a crucial link in a spiritual chain, a runner in a generational relay race. The baton of faith and wisdom you carry today must be passed on with intentionality and purpose. The race for the Kingdom continues through those you've equipped, empowered, and entrusted. This is a sobering and beautiful truth. It means that your role isn't to be the final destination, but the launching pad for the next generation of builders.

Don't just think about what you're building. Think about who's watching you build it. Think about your children, your spouse, your team, your church, and your community. The integrity of your daily decisions, the consistency of your faith, and the quiet strength of your obedience aren't just personal attributes. They're all seeds being planted in the soil of someone else's future. The way you handle success, the way you respond to failure, and the way you treat people, all of this becomes a part of the legacy you're leaving behind. A life lived for legacy is a life lived in constant awareness of the impact on others.

Don't Let It Die with You

Don't make the tragic mistake of hoarding what God has taught you. Too many leaders, entrepreneurs, and parents die with their hard-won secrets still locked inside them. They take their lessons learned the hard way, truths forged in failure, and blueprints revealed through prayer and obedience, with them to the grave. Kingdom legacy requires more than just living a good life; it requires transferring your wisdom and experience well.

The next generation doesn't just need our encouragement; they need our instruction. They need us to open our playbooks and show them how the game is played. Let your ceiling become their floor by passing down the tools that helped you reach it. Share your scars, not just your successes. Share your stories of failure, not just your stories of victory. Share your systems and your strategies. Real legacy doesn't hide its insights to maintain a competitive advantage. It hands them over with a spirit of generosity and an intentional desire to see others succeed.

Your scars may be the very blueprint someone else needs. Your toughest seasons might become someone else's survival guide. If God brought you through it, there's someone waiting on the other side of your testimony to know that victory is possible.

Legacy Over Likes in Business

For the Kingdom entrepreneur, this principle is particularly powerful. You must think generationally in your business. You're not just creating a product or a service. You're building a culture, establishing a set of values, and modeling a way of doing business that can be carried forward. When profit is prioritized over purpose, the business is a fragile, self-centered entity that often dies with you. However, when purpose is so deeply woven into your leadership, your systems, and your service, your impact echoes far beyond your lifetime.

Legacy in business means training leaders, not just hiring workers. It means pouring into the character of your team, not just tracking their productivity. It means building a reputation that honors God, even if it costs you short-term financial gain. Sometimes legacy means walking away from a shortcut, even when no one would've known. Heaven always knows. Heaven always rewards. It means making a decision not based on what will give you the most likes today, but what will build the most trust tomorrow.

I know a businessman who has grown his real estate business into a multi-million dollar company. He didn't do anything glamorous. In fact, he did the opposite. He quietly poured into people. He allowed his faith in God to direct his steps and his actions. His deliberate integrity meant God received the glory, and those around him saw the reflection of Christ. This man never sought fortune the way most do, but he found it through the same principles outlined throughout Kingdom Hustle. He didn't chase a platform. He lived with purpose. His legacy speaks louder than any marketing campaign ever could.

Forgotten by Men, Remembered by God

Scripture is filled with powerful examples of men and women who never sought fame but left an indelible legacy. Noah obeyed when it had never rained, building an ark in a world that mocked him. Ruth stayed loyal to her mother-in-law when she had nothing to gain and everything to lose, and her faithfulness became a link in the lineage of Christ. Joseph stewarded the entire nation of Egypt through a severe famine, not for his own comfort or gain, but to preserve a nation and, in doing so, to save the very people of God. They weren't chasing influence. They were fulfilling an assignment. Because they were faithful to their assignment, we're still talking about them today.

We remember names like Nehemiah, not because he built something flashy or became a celebrity, but because he refused to come down from the wall. He understood the value of the unseen, the sacredness of the task God had given him, and the high cost of distraction. His response to his critics and distractors is a timeless mantra for any Kingdom builder: *"I am carrying on a great project and cannot go down. Why should the work stop while I leave it and go down to you?" — Nehemiah 6:3.*

You, too, must learn to say this. There are distractions, opportunities, and temptations that will try to lure you down from your wall, the wall of faithfulness, integrity, and purpose. Legacy is built by those who stay on the wall, even when it's uncomfortable and unseen.

Your Name Will Be Forgotten, But Not Your Fruit

One day, your website will expire. Your email list will fade. Your logo will be replaced. Yet, your obedience will live on. The people you discipled, the prayers you prayed, the sacrifices you made, and the truth you stood on, those things don't die. They multiply. They get passed on to the next generation, who then pass them on to the one after that.

That's the Kingdom way of doing things. Not addition, but multiplication. A legacy builder doesn't ask, "How much can I gather?" but "What can I give that will outlive me?" Your life isn't a vessel to be filled; it's a seed to be planted. Plant it well, with intention, and with eternity in mind.

Kingdom Challenge: Build Like It's Not About You

I challenge you to ask God to show you where you've been living for likes instead of legacy. Are you building to be seen, or building what will stand?

Have a conversation with someone younger than you and pour into them without expecting anything back.

Commit to leaving a trail, not a platform. Platforms can fall, but trails lead somewhere, guiding those who come after you.

Remember, it's not about being remembered. It's about leaving something behind worth remembering.

WALK IT OUT

Leaving A Lasting Fire

To leave a lasting fire is to live with legacy in mind. Kingdom builders understand that the true measure of success is not what they achieve, but what continues after they're gone. Begin by asking God to show you who needs what He has placed in you. Identify the people, teams, or communities you can invest in. Teach them not only what you know, but how to carry the heart behind it. Passing on wisdom keeps the flame alive long after your season changes.

Be intentional about documentation. Write down the lessons, stories, and principles that shaped your journey. A journal today becomes a guide for someone tomorrow. Record what God taught you in seasons of breakthrough and seasons of testing. Legacy is preserved through written truth as much as spoken example.

Model consistency for those who watch you. Let them see humility in your victories and grace in your challenges. Influence is sustained not through perfection, but through integrity. When others witness steadiness under pressure, they learn that faith works in every circumstance.

Invest time where it matters most. Mentorship rarely happens on stages; it's formed in conversations, in quiet prayers, in shared moments of encouragement. Prioritize people over projects. Build systems that allow others to thrive without needing your constant oversight. When you lead this way, the Kingdom expands through generations, not just achievements.

Leaving a lasting fire means living in such a way that others see Christ's light in you and learn how to keep it burning in themselves. Your words, your work, and your worship become fuel for those who follow. When your story is finished, the fire remains; lighting paths, igniting purpose, and continuing the work you began for the glory of the King.

THE COMMISSIONING

Your life isn't a side hustle; it's a Kingdom hustle, commissioned by God, anointed for eternal impact, and built for a purpose that stretches into eternity.

The world will tell you to compartmentalize, to keep your faith private, to chase success, accumulate more, to hustle harder to get ahead. The Kingdom tells a different story. You were created to integrate, not separate, your faith and your work. You were created to hustle for what matters most, and to measure success not by scale, but by surrender.

This book was never an invitation to grind harder in your own strength. It's been a call to go deeper in your relationship with the King. To lead from a place of intimacy; to build with Heaven's blueprint, and to stop striving for human applause and start faithfully stewarding your divine assignment.

Some of you will raise children with quiet consistency and faithfulness; one of the toughest, yet greatest, assignments. Some of you will plant churches. Still, others will influence boardrooms, job sites, classrooms, or small-town storefronts. The platforms may be vastly different, but the purpose remains the same: build faithfully, love deeply, and glorify God in every corner of your hustle.

The true call of Kingdom hustle is not about what you build. It's about who you become while you build it.

Will you be the builder who burns out chasing applause, or the steward who builds with peace?

Will you spend your life hustling for attention, or will you leverage your life for eternal impact?

Will you climb the ladder of worldly success only to find your soul empty at the top, or will you stay rooted in purpose and walk with joy, even when the world overlooks you?

You don't have to strive to prove yourself to anyone. You're already called, already chosen, and already loved by the King.

"... choose for yourselves this day whom you will serve, ... But as for me and my household, we will serve the Lord." —Joshua 24:15

When your race is finished, may your life echo far beyond your time, not because you made a name for yourself, but because you faithfully bore the name of the One who sent you.

Now go.
Build what matters.
Lead with courage.
Serve with humility.
Hustle with eternity in your heart.

This is your commissioning.

Walk in it.

ABOUT THE AUTHOR

Derek Stone is a faith-driven entrepreneur, business owner, small group leader, and co-host of *The Arc Entrepreneur Podcast*.

As the owner of Duncan Custom Gutter & Copper Craft, he leads with integrity, excellence, and a Christ-centered vision. Derek is passionate about raising up a generation of entrepreneurs who build with purpose over profit and keep eternity in focus. He lives in Florida with his wife, Alicia, and their 5 children.

www.ingramcontent.com/pod-product-compliance
Lightning Source LLC
Chambersburg PA
CBHW060326050426
42449CB00011B/2664